en ou gh.

LIVING A LIFE BEYOND PERFORMANCE

I0211906

Copyright © 2024 by Ben Dailey and Travis Hall

Published by Arrows & Stones

All rights reserved. No portion of this book may be reproduced, stored in a retrieval system, or transmitted in any form or by any means—electronic, mechanical, photocopy, recording, scanning, or other—except for brief quotations in critical reviews or articles, without prior written permission of the author.

Unless otherwise noted, all Scripture quotations are taken from the ESV® Bible (The Holy Bible, English Standard Version®), copyright © 2001 by Crossway, a publishing ministry of Good News Publishers. Used by permission. All rights reserved. | Scripture quotations marked AMP are taken from the Amplified® Bible (AMP), Copyright © 2015 by The Lockman Foundation. Used by permission. www.lockman.org | Scripture quotations marked NIV are taken from the Holy Bible, New International Version®, NIV®. Copyright © 1973, 1978, 1984, 2011 by Biblica, Inc.™ Used by permission of Zondervan. All rights reserved worldwide. www.zondervan.com. The "NIV" and "New International Version" are trademarks registered in the United States Patent and Trademark Office by Biblica, Inc.™ | Scripture quotations marked NKJV are taken from the New King James Version®. Copyright © 1982 by Thomas Nelson. Used by permission. All rights reserved. | Scripture quotations marked TPT are from The Passion Translation®. Copyright © 2017, 2018 by Passion & Fire Ministries, Inc. Used by permission. All rights reserved. ThePassionTranslation.com.

For foreign and subsidiary rights, contact the author.

Cover design by Kim Dailey
Ben Dailey photo by Morgan Archer
Travis Hall photo by Lyndsey Hobby

ISBN: 978-1-957369-62-4   1 2 3 4 5 6 7 8 9 10

Printed in the United States of America

enough.

LIVING A LIFE BEYOND PERFORMANCE

BEN DAILEY & TRAVIS HALL

ARROWS & STONES

OTHER BOOKS BY BEN DAILEY & TRAVIS HALL:

Collide

Limitless

Captured By Grace

7 Deadly Thoughts

Stop Arguing Start Communicating

Dedication from Ben:
To Steve and Kendra Chaney, Managing Partner,
Chaney & Associates, APC. Your belief in the message
of the gospel and your support for this book has
played a pivotal role in bringing this work to life. Your
generosity will forever resonate within these pages,
reminding readers of the goodness and favor of God.

Thank you for making this journey possible.

Dedication from Travis:
To my children, Travis, Randy, Elijah,
Grace, Savannah, and Olivia. I love you.
I'm proud of you. You are enough.

CONTENTS

AN INTRODUCTION TO THE AUTHORS

BEN DAILEY is the Lead Pastor of Calvary Church in the Dallas area. He is known for his love for the gospel, his creative style of communication, and his unconventional ministry strategy. The church is one of the most culturally diverse congregations in the nation. Ben is the author of *Collide: When Your Desires Meet God's Heart, Limitless: The Life You Were Meant to Live,* and *Captured by Grace: Be Freed from Fear so You Can Really Live!* He oversees Gospel Circle of Churches and other gospel-centered ministries for pastors and church leaders.

Ben and his wife Kim have two married children: Kyla and Marcy, and Kade and Jada.

TRAVIS HALL is an ordained bishop in the Church of God and the Lead Pastor of Life Church International in the Atlanta area. He is passionate about equipping leaders to start well, stay well, and finish well, communicating the gospel of grace, and reaching people who are far from God. He is the author of *7 Deadly Thoughts: Conquer the Thoughts that Limit Your Life*.

Travis and his wife, Tina, have four children.

We are writing this book together because over the past six years, we've become close friends and "partners in the gospel". Our relationship has pushed us to explore the grace of God more deeply and find a different—more joyful yet more powerful— motivation to live every moment for the One who has demonstrated such amazing love for us. Our stories are central to this book, so we'll identify which of us is telling our stories. Besides those, we share every concept, every principle, and every blessing we communicate about the gospel of grace.

Christ is our message! We preach to awaken hearts and bring every person into the full understanding of truth. It has become my inspiration and passion in ministry to labor with a tireless intensity, with His power flowing through me, to present to every believer the revelation of being His perfect one in Jesus Christ (Colossians 1:28-29, TPT).

PART 1

I've Had Enough!

We're using punctuation for the chapters in each of the four parts of this book. The first one is an exclamation point, demonstrating that change comes when we come to the end of ourselves . . . when we've had enough of trying so hard to measure up.

CHAPTER 1

THIS CAN'T BE REAL!

I LIED. I (TRAVIS) AM A PASTOR. I KNEW BETTER, BUT I desperately wanted a way out. Let me back up and tell you what happened.

In 2017, I saw Ben's Instagram post about his leadership strategy. The subject is very important to me, so I sent him a DM asking him for more information. I received a text with a phone number. I assumed it was his assistant, but when I called, to my surprise, it was Ben himself. Very soon we had a conversation over Facetime. It was all about identifying and equipping leaders, but in a subsequent conversation a week or two later, he mentioned something about grace being the most powerful motivation for leaders. I thought, *That's nice*, but I didn't pay much attention to it. After all, what does grace have to do with a leadership strategy?

I had known Ben for only a couple of months when he invited me to come to a leadership event at Calvary, his church in Dallas. I've been to enough pastors' events to have realistic expectations about them. Pastors don't make friends there; they make connections. My wife Tina encouraged me to go because it might be good to meet pastors from across the country.

When I told Ben I was coming, he seemed genuinely excited. To be honest, his response felt odd to me. I was going to be just one more pastor sitting in one more chair listening to another leadership talk, meeting a few more pastors. Ben's enthusiasm caused me to put up my guard. I assumed, *He wants something from me. I don't know what it is, but I'd better be careful.*

From the moment one of the staff members picked me up at the airport—from dinner that night with some other pastors, to casual conversations and talks about leadership—something felt strange . . . off . . . weird, but I couldn't put my finger on it. My antennae were up: I watched how Ben and his team interacted with each other, and I noticed how they treated me and the other pastors. Their authenticity and kindness on such a large scale were both rich and rare. It was very unsettling.

That night at the hotel, I called Tina. She asked, "How did it go today?"

"Different. Very different."

"What do you mean?" she asked.

"I don't know. I haven't figured it out yet."

She probed, "Different good or different bad?"

"I can't tell yet. Maybe I'll know more tomorrow."

The next morning during the worship and teaching, my soul felt agitated—not because the Holy Spirit had given me discernment about some sin. It wasn't that at all. I felt unnerved because I didn't have a shelf to put this experience on. I was confused, off balance, wondering what in the world was going on with these people. There was the presence of genuine care for one another, but there was also the absence of game-playing, posing, power plays, competition, comparison, and jockeying for position. At most pastors' events, I didn't see people genuinely enjoying each other; I saw them desperately trying to prove they belong. That was the air I'd been breathing for decades. It may have been smog, but without it, I was suffocating. But these people weren't looking past me to find someone more important they could impress. They were looking at me!

As we broke for lunch, I called my administrative assistant at my church and told her, "Get me on the first flight home." She started to ask a question, but I interrupted, "I just need to get home. I shouldn't have come. The people here are strange. I don't care what you need to do, just get me on a flight as soon as you can." She found a flight that left in a couple of hours.

I went back to my room, packed, and called an Uber. On the way to the airport, I got a call. It was Ben. I had been sure no one would notice that I'd left, but Ben did. He asked, "Hey, I want to introduce you to some people. Where are you?"

That's when I lied. "I've got something going on at home, so I have to get back. My wife needs me. It's really important that I get back as soon as possible. Sorry about leaving early."

Ben said, "Oh, okay. Glad you could come. I hope things work out at home." And we hung up.

A few minutes later, it became obvious that Ben wasn't buying my line. I got a short text that said only, "You mad, bro?"

I lied again: "No, I'm good. Just have to get back."

In the days after I got home, I remembered a time when I was a kid and my mother took me to church for the first time that wasn't Christmas or Easter. It was a Spirit-filled church in Saginaw, Michigan. During the service, someone spoke in tongues. I reached over and tugged on my mom's shirt and whispered, "What's that?"

She shook her head and mouthed, "I don't know."

I couldn't explain it, but I couldn't shake it. I kept thinking about it until we went back to that church and discovered that it happens all the time. For me, it was odd and unsettling; for them, it was completely normal. In the same way, I couldn't explain what I'd sensed at Ben's pastors' conference, but I couldn't shake it either.

Ben didn't give up on me. I'm pretty sure he knew I hadn't been honest with him about the reason I left the event, but he kept calling and texting, and he sent me his book, *Limitless*.[1] Gradually, I was able to find words that described what I was feeling. I began to realize that what I'd felt in that room at Ben's church was a level of freedom, authenticity, love, and grace I'd never felt before.

But I was still very guarded. I wasn't used to new relationships that weren't at least a little manipulative, where someone didn't want something from me. I assumed Ben had some kind of angle, but up to this point, I couldn't find it. He seemed to be genuine, but I was still skeptical. I think I have a pretty good antenna for detecting phoniness, and I was frustrated that I couldn't see through Ben's motives. At one point about six months later, Ben was passing through Atlanta and we met for breakfast. I couldn't

---

1   Ben Dailey, *Limitless: The Life You Were Meant to Live* (Salubris Resources, 2016).

take it anymore so I asked Ben bluntly, "What do you want from me? If you want our church to become one of your locations, that's not going to happen!"

He looked at me and said, "Nothing." I still didn't believe him, but his consistent kindness gradually eroded the high walls of my defensiveness. He was honest, vulnerable about his own struggles, and not hiding to protect his image or posing to impress me.

Ben invited me to another event at Calvary, and this time, I was able to put the pieces together: What I'd experienced from all the people there was what they were experiencing in their relationship with Ben: a culture of grace, love, and freedom to be all God called them to be. It had been confusing and, to be honest, a little repulsive because I still had trouble believing it was true, but gradually, it became life and breath. For years, I hadn't even had the self-awareness to ask, "Is it possible to live, love, and serve only because of the grace of God?" I now had the answer.

DECEIVING OTHERS BECOMES A HABIT WHEN WE'VE DECEIVED OURSELVES SO MUCH AND FOR SO LONG THAT WE AREN'T SURE WHAT'S TRUE ANY LONGER.

For me the beginning of the journey of healing wasn't like putting a Band-Aid on a scrape; it was like being picked up off the side of the road by EMS when I had multiple compound fractures. The wounds were deep and raw, and the lie I told Ben when I left early was just one in a pattern of lies. For years, I never felt I was quite enough—not quite acceptable, not quite adequate, not quite lovable. The sense that I was defective was bad enough, but as a Christian, I'd been told that "we're overcomers" and we have "victory in Jesus." I believed those statements with all my heart, but deep in my soul, I felt "less than". No matter how hard I tried, my very best performance wasn't enough . . . and I tried really hard. Over the years, I created a persona, an image of who I thought I should be and who other people expected me to be. When people asked me how I was doing, I always said something like, "Great, and getting even better!" I told people that I was happy and fulfilled, but my thoughts were plagued with self-doubt and frustration. Deceiving others becomes a habit when we've deceived ourselves so much and for so long that we aren't sure what's true any longer. The novelist Fyodor Dostoevsky gave good advice:

> Above all, don't lie to yourself. The man who lies to himself and listens to his own lie comes to a point that he cannot distinguish the truth within him, or around him, and so loses all respect for himself and for others. And having no respect, he ceases to love.[2]

We're pastors, but our experiences aren't unique. As we meet with good-hearted believers in our churches and in our travels across the country, we find countless people who identify with the pain and confusion created by a performance-driven identity. They wholeheartedly embrace the truth of God's love, forgiveness, and acceptance, but it hasn't penetrated into the recesses of their hearts.

---

2   Fyodor Dostoevsky, *The Brothers Karamazou*, cited in *Before You Hit Send,* by Dr. Emerson Eggerichs, p. 26.

We live in a world of comparison. When we're performing better than others, we feel good about ourselves, but when we fail (or when others succeed more than we do), we berate ourselves for being inferior . . . and we can't stand to be inferior! We hear the voice of a harsh inner critic, condemning us and telling us we're worthless, helpless, and hopeless; no one could possibly like us, much less love us; we're alone because we're so defective; and our only hope is to try even harder to perform to win approval.

But there's another voice—the voice of the Good Shepherd. As we'll see in the pages of this book, the Bible isn't shy about the supernatural power of the grace of God. To the one who believes, "I can't ever do enough," Jesus says, "I've done it all. *Tetelestai*. It is finished." To the one who feels unloved and unlovable, Jesus says, "You're my treasure, my delight." To the one who feels defective, Jesus says, "In me, you have everything you will ever need." To the one who feels like an orphan, Jesus says, "You're adopted by the Father, and he is thrilled to call you his own."

Yes, we know that you probably already know these things, so why is it so hard for these truths to capture our hearts, melt us in the love of God, and transform us from the inside out? Thanks for asking. That's what this book is about. It's one thing to be told that honey is sweet, but it's something quite different to taste its delectable sweetness. We're inviting you to taste the sweetness of the grace of God.

At the end of each chapter, you'll find some questions to stimulate deeper reflection and provide direction for prayer. You can also use these in team meetings, small groups, and other gatherings with friends who long to experience God's amazing grace.

Don't rush through them. This isn't a speed drill. Take your time and ask God to speak to you.

THINK ABOUT IT:

» *What are some reasons why being performance-driven instead of grace-led is so common?*

» *What are different ways trying to perform well enough to be accepted affects people? How has it affected you?*

» *What do you hope to get out of this book?*

CHAPTER 2

GET ON THE RIGHT CYCLE!

WE LEARN BY CONTRASTS: THIS AND NOT THAT. LIFE is about choices, but to make good ones, we need to see the clear alternatives. For believers, there are two very different ways to live: the cycle of never enough . . . and the cycle of enough.

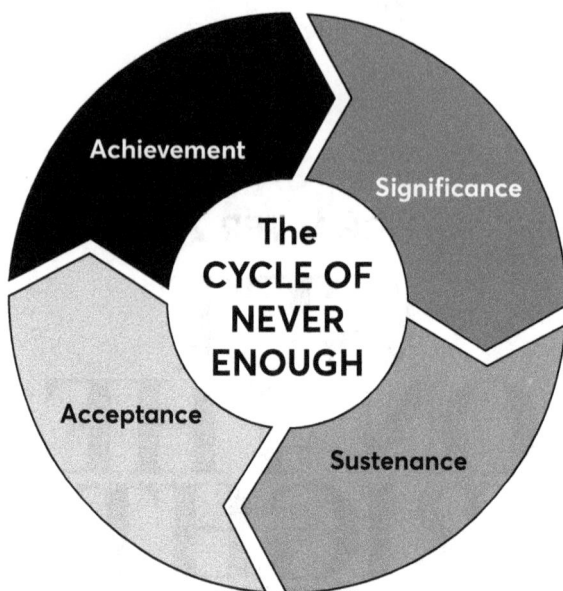

The CYCLE OF NEVER ENOUGH

Achievement — Significance — Sustenance — Acceptance

» **Achievement:** Achieve is enough to prove to myself and others that I am enough.
» **Significance:** Gain a sense of significance (identity, worth, and platform) so I'll get. . .
» **Sustenance:** If I accumulate enough money, power, fame, or admiration, I'll finally accomplish the one thing I've been searching for. . .
» **Acceptance:** Finally, I feel like I am enough (but it never lasts, and eventually, the cycle starts all over again).

It should sound pretty familiar because that's the way the vast majority of people in our culture—as well as most of the people in our churches—live. The pressing goal is to be enough, to feel like we're enough, to finally get to a point where we're successful and accepted enough to fill the gaping hole in our hearts . . . but it's all a pipedream. It's never enough.

FOR BELIEVERS, STRIVING ISN'T THE PROBLEM; EARNING IS THE PROBLEM.

But there's another—in fact, a totally different—way to live.

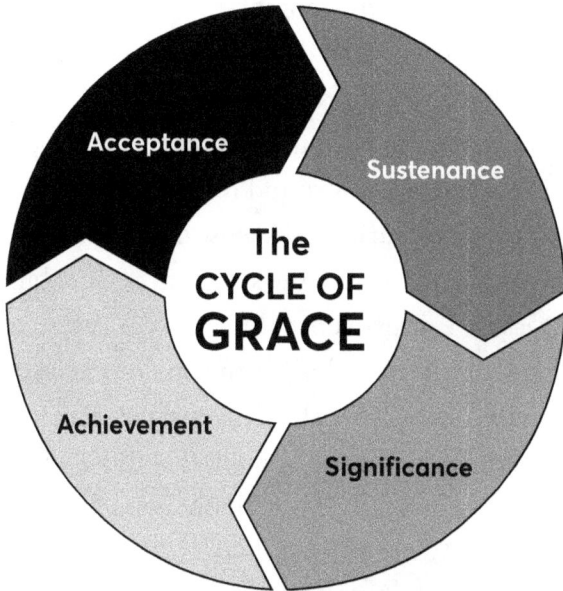

Here, we start with complete, total, wonderful acceptance, not earned by performance but given by grace.

» **Acceptance:** Grace starts where striving ends. Because of our faith in what Jesus accomplished on the cross—you are accepted (Ephesians1:6-7)!

» **Sustenance:** You discover that everything you need is found in Christ. Physically, mentally, emotionally, and spiritually, Jesus sustains us—He is our source.

» **Significance:** You don't need a platform, titles, fame, or fortune to be significant. God the Father thinks you're so significant that He sent His Son to die on the cross. Significance is found in Christ alone.

» **Achievement:** At this point in the Cycle of enoughness, you are finally free to achieve your God-given purpose without hindrance becauseyou know you're achieving from your acceptance rather than for it.

For believers, *striving* isn't the problem; *earning* is the problem. When we believe our efforts somehow earn points with God, we'll never *be* enough; we'll never *have* enough; we'll never *do* enough. But when we believe and receive the gospel of grace, it gives us enormous security and a sense of significance. The result is that we work hard to build the kingdom of God, but for a very different reason. Paul explained this principle in his second letter to the Christians in Corinth: "For the love of Christ controls us, because we have concluded this: that one has died for all, therefore all have died; and he died for all, that those who live might no longer live for themselves but for him who for their sake died and was raised" (2 Corinthians 5:14-15, ESV). We live, serve, and lead with far different motives than comparison and competition ... or trying to prove we're valuable to God and others. "The love of Christ controls," energizes, and directs us.

My (Ben's) revelation of the power of the gospel began at the end of 2012. For several years, I kept growing and learning. It was the most liberating time I'd ever known! As the calendar turned to 2020, I told my wife Kim that it was time for me to go even deeper with Jesus. My sense of need didn't come out of thin air. God often uses heartaches and struggles to take us to a deeper level of dependence, and during those months, I'd gone through a series of deep relational heartaches ... and then early rumors of a virus out of China became all too real and changed everything. I felt like my soul was a ball of strings. When I pulled on one, it grabbed a bunch of others and formed knots. The Lord surfaced old feelings and beliefs that had haunted me before, and now he was inviting me to deal with them more conclusively. The recent years of experiencing God's grace gave me the strength and confidence to look in the mirror and be more honest than ever before. But I knew it wasn't going to be easy or pleasant. I had a choice: to push those emotions and thoughts back down into the abyss of my heart and hope they go away . . . or take them to the throne of grace and deal with them. The adversity outside me forced me to be more honest about the wounds inside me.

The image that came through during that time is that God is the gardener, and my heart is his garden. With patience, care, and wisdom, he pulled up weeds, planted seeds, and pruned healthy vines—not to hurt me but to help me grow. I had been thrilled by the love of Jesus over the previous few years, but I began to experience his tenderness, his presence, and his delight in fresh and deeper ways. More than ever, I'm learning to rest— not to stop working but to stop striving so hard to make things happen. I'm learning to trust that God is in control of the harvest, and I'm not. And I'm learning that in him, I'm enough— hearing far less of the voice of the inner critic, experiencing far less anxiety about getting things done, and suffering far less insecurity from comparing myself with others. I'm more present with Kim and the kids, less worried about outcomes, and more passionate about Christ and his kingdom. Thank God for his patience and kindness in my life!

Travis and I want to be honest and make some confessions at the beginning of this book:

» We were addicted to performing to earn approval (and sometimes we still fall off the wagon).

» We have believed in the finished work of Christ for many years, but somehow, this truth didn't go deep enough.

» We're pastors, but we're just like you, with the same misunderstandings and temptations.

» We're still on the journey of learning and unlearning, healing, and maturing.

We're writing this book because the true message of the gospel has transformed us. It has given us more joy, love, and life than we ever dreamed possible, and we want to share it with you. We're inviting you to join us on this journey away from performance-based living and into the wonder of being fully known and fully loved by God. In the four parts of the book, we'll circle back to the foundational truths and applications of grace—not because we couldn't think of anything else to say, but because the scriptures circle back to them over and over again. We need to see and experience grace from every conceivable angle, and this is more important than anything else we'll ever learn.

Buckle up! This journey is going to be more thrilling than you ever imagined . . . but probably more threatening than you ever feared. After Paul saw Jesus on the road to Damascus, he was led to the city where a man named Ananias met him. He told Paul, "'Brother Saul, the Lord Jesus who appeared to you on the road by which you came has sent me so that you may regain your sight and be filled with the Holy Spirit.' And immediately something like scales fell from his eyes, and he regained his sight" (Acts

9:17-18, ESV). It took a miracle of God for the scales to fall from Paul's eyes so that he could see God's grace more clearly, and we trust God will perform the same miracle for you.

Yes, the wonder of grace certainly *is* real!

THINK ABOUT IT:

» *What are some of the messages of the harsh inner critic? What impact do they have?*

» *If change comes only when we give up on unworkable strategies such as trying so hard to measure up, how close are you to that point? Explain your answer.*

» *On a scale of 0 (not at all) to 10 (to the max), how real has your experience of God's grace been in the past month or so?*

CHAPTER 3

ENOUGH IS ENOUGH! . . . LUTHER'S PERSPECTIVE

I (TRAVIS) GOT A PHONE CALL FROM A FRIEND WHO IS a pastor. He said, "I'm on my way home from seeing my counselor, and I wanted to tell you what I discovered today. First, I want to thank you for being so clear and consistent in communicating the message of grace and the New Covenant. Today, as I talked to my counselor, I realized that what I thought was the gospel—which was based on performance, not grace—hadn't set me free at all. In fact, it has been the source of tremendous trauma in my life."

A week later, I talked to my friend again. He was so excited that he almost climbed through the phone to tell me, "Travis, where have I been for so long? How could I have missed it so badly? I'm beginning to understand that the gospel really is good news!" He explained that he had to unlearn the carefully constructed but false teaching that yes, God loves us, but he only *really* loves us when we perform with perfection, which, of course, is an unreachable target. Since childhood, he had lived with the nagging sense that no matter how hard he tried, he couldn't really measure up. To him, grace was God's "get out of jail" card. It meant that he was forgiven, but he'd better try harder the next time if he wanted to keep the love of God that he had worked so hard to earn.

What led my friend to go to a counselor? He had finally had enough. He had tried incredibly hard to meet God's standards, but it led him to a rollercoaster of self-righteousness when he thought he was doing well and self-condemnation and shame when he wasn't . . . which, as it is for many of us, was quite often. Shame had become the prison of his soul, and for a long time, he assumed the sentence was life without parole.

My friend isn't alone. In fact, Ben and I believe the vast majority of people who consider themselves to be Christians (and we aren't disputing this claim at all) live under the dark cloud of believing their performance determines God's love, forgiveness, and acceptance. They may intellectually affirm the message of New Covenant grace, but they live under the weight of Old Covenant rules, regulations, judgment, and punishment.

THOSE OF US WHO HAVEN'T BEEN CAPTURED BY GRACE ARE CHRONICALLY AND RADICALLY INSECURE.

We can identify three streams that lead into the Dead Sea of performance-based living.

First, legalism is the belief that trying to achieve perfection through the law and unspoken church rules earns points with God. This was more of a problem a few decades ago when these rules were very clearly articulated and enforced by upturned noses, sideways glances, and isolation. The rules concerned almost every aspect of life: what we wore, where we went, the words we used, the version of the Bible we read, the movies we saw, and on and on. We were more like Pharisees than disciples of Jesus. In recent years, however, Christians have paddled into a second stream: moralism. Instead of clear and strict rules, this is the belief that if we're pretty good people (whatever that might mean), we're acceptable to God. We might think of legalism as a teacher with a very strict grading system, and moralism is grading on a curve. But there's a third stream that flows into the cesspool of self-righteousness and self-condemnation: human nature. The human heart runs on the desire to prove ourselves like our cars run on gas. We can even say that many people don't even want grace because it means they have to depend on someone else for their security and value! Most of us have difficulty believing that our hearts lean hard toward performance. After all, we sing the hymns, read the Bible, and pray the prayers. Doesn't that show that we trust in God's amazing grace? No, not necessarily.

Those of us who haven't been captured by grace are chronically and radically insecure. When we walk into a room, we check out where we are in the pecking order. We want to see who accepts us, who competes with us for attention, and who makes us look inferior. Living to impress others is slowly exhausting because the impression has to be reinforced time after time—we're always auditioning, hoping we get the part. No matter how many people we impress, it only satisfies for a short time because the gnawing emptiness and relentless drive propel us to try to impress someone a little higher, a little smarter, a little stronger. In interactions, we magnify our strengths and minimize our weaknesses. We look for ways to say and do just the right thing. We're always on stage. We smile, we try to be wise, we laugh, but if we peel back the façade, we realize it's all just a game.

> ## THE IRONY IS THAT WE WANT PEOPLE WHO DON'T KNOW WHO THEY ARE TO TELL US WHO WE ARE.

When our hearts allow us to be honest, we ask, "Am I enough? Will I ever be enough?" As we'll see, these are the normal questions of the human heart, and they can lead to surprising answers. In fact, Jesus faced questions very much like these. When John was preaching repentance and baptizing people in the Jordan, Jesus came to be baptized. John was reluctant because he knew that Jesus was much greater than him. Jesus convinced him that it was the right thing to do. Matthew tells us,

> And when Jesus was baptized, immediately he went up from the water, and behold, the heavens were opened to him, and he saw the Spirit of God descending like a dove and coming to rest on him; and behold, a voice from heaven said, 'This is my beloved Son, with whom I am well pleased.'" —Matthew 3:16-17

Notice that the Father affirmed him, accepted him, and was "well pleased" with him before he did anything for the kingdom. Acceptance preceded performance.

Immediately, the Spirit led Jesus into the wilderness to be tempted by the devil. The revelation of Jesus's identity was followed by the temptation to deny that identity, but when he passed the test, it led to his elevation. Matthew records three specific temptations, and all of them questioned Jesus's identity and security:

1) The first temptation: Jesus had fasted for forty days and nights, and then the devil told him, ". . . If you are the Son of God, command these stones to become loaves of bread" (Matthew 4:3). The devil wanted Jesus to perform to meet his own needs. This is the lie, "You are what you do." For us, it's the drive to prove ourselves by our successes. We live in dread of any kind of failure because it means we're worthless. We believe, "The more I accomplish, the more I'm somebody." Many of us are emotionally and relationally killing ourselves trying to turn stones into bread because we believe our doing proves our value. The gospel says that Jesus is the Bread of Life, and when we feed on his love, forgiveness, and acceptance, we're filled and satisfied. His provision is enough.

2) The second temptation: The devil took Jesus to the pinnacle of the temple in Jerusalem, and he said, ". . . If you are the Son of God, throw yourself down, for it is written, 'He will command his angels concerning you'" (vs. 6). The temple was a high-profile place. All of the important leaders of influence would have been there. He wanted Jesus to impress people

with a miracle. This is the lie: You are what people think of you. For us, it's the temptation to live for the smiles and applause of other people. Our value is seen in the faces of people instead of the face of God, which makes us radically insecure, changing our opinions to please the person in front of us. The irony is that we want people who don't know who they are to tell us who we are. The gospel tells us that God's opinion of us is infinitely more important than anyone else's, and he adores us. His smile is enough.

3) The third temptation: Satan then took Jesus to a mountain and showed him the kingdoms of the world. He told Jesus, "'All these I will give you, if you will fall down and worship me'" (vs. 8-9). The lie: You are what you have. He wanted Jesus to build his kingdom and have power and glory apart from the Father. He wouldn't have to face the cross, and he wouldn't have to wait. For us, it's the compulsion to acquire more and more stuff, to leave the place of peace, rest, and gratitude to try to fill the hole in our hearts with bigger and better . . . always bigger and better. We believe, "The more I have, the more I am." But in the end, if I am what I have then I can never have enough to feel like I'm enough. The gospel tells us that only Jesus can fill that hole, and he fills it to overflowing. His power, peace, and purpose are enough.

These are our temptations, too. Basing our identity on performance, possessions, and power is the way the world operates all day every day in every sphere . . . except one: in our relationship with God. To embrace grace, we have to fight the temptations to perform to meet our own needs, to prove ourselves to others, and to create an identity based on our wealth, intelligence, and strength. Satan continually asks us, "If you want security, status, and significance, are you willing to do whatever it takes to impress people who are watching you?" Far too often, our answer is "Yes!"

The gospel of grace is both forensic and relational. When we pray, "Our Father who is in heaven," three things must have taken place for us to call him our Father. The doctrine of justification includes two of them: If we are "in Christ," his death is credited to us to pay for all our sins, and his righteous life is credited to us so that we are declared righteous in his sight. The forensic, legal aspects of justification lead to a third crucial truth: God delights in making us his own! God has adopted us into his family. When a child is adopted in most states, the judge declares that the adoptive parents may disinherit their natural children, but they can't disinherit their adopted child. The child is absolutely secure in the new family. In his letter to the Romans, Paul assured them,

> For all who are led by the Spirit of God are sons of God. For you did not receive the spirit of slavery to fall back into fear, but you have received the Spirit of adoption as sons, by whom we cry, 'Abba! Father!' The Spirit himself bears witness with our spirit that we are children of God, and if children, then heirs—heirs of God and fellow heirs with Christ . . .—Romans 8:14-17

(We'll examine these truths in more detail later in the book.)

To live in the truth of the gospel of grace, we have to do the hard work to unlearn legalism and moralism, and we have to fight against our natural instincts to earn security and status. Does this matter? You bet it does! A recent study on "Grace, Legalism, and Mental Health" makes a direct correlation between the understanding of New Covenant grace and overall well-being. The study reports that those who take a more legalistic approach to God suffer more "depression, anxiety, scrupulosity (religious obsessive-compulsive disorder), perfectionism, and shame."[3] When these efforts fail (which is inevitable), people double down, trying even harder and following the rules more diligently until, at some point, they give up. At that moment, some walk away from the faith because "it didn't work," but others find liberation, stability, and joy in an experience of the grace of God. They gave up on performance as the foundation of their lives, but they didn't give up on God.

The study could have looked at insights from Martin Luther five centuries ago. He came to a similar conclusion:

> The more someone tries to bring peace to his conscience through his own righteousness, the more disquieted he makes it. I went to confession frequently, and I performed the assigned penances faithfully. Nevertheless, my conscience could never achieve certainty but was always in doubt. . . . the longer I tried to heal my uncertain, weak, and troubled conscience with human traditions, the more uncertain, weak, and troubled I continually made it. In this way, by observing human traditions, I transgressed them even more; and by following the righteousness of the monastic order, I was never able to reach it.[4]

You don't have to be a guilt-ridden, sixteenth-century German monk to miss the message of unconditional grace. A study by the American Psychological Association looked at the contrasting impacts of "conditional grace", which is based on performance,

---

3   Daniel K. Judd, W. Justin Dyer, and Justin B. Top, *Grace, Legalism, and Mental Health: Examining Direct and Mediating Relationships* (American Psychological Association: Provo, Utah, 2018).
4   Martin Luther, *Luther's Works: Lectures on Galatians, Vol. 27* (Concordia Publishing House: St. Louis, 1999).

and "unconditional grace", which can only be received as a gift. The authors reported:

> Results indicated that grace received from works [i.e., performance] predicted less gratitude, physical and mental health, and greater belief in a punishing God, depression, negative affect [or mood], extrinsic religious orientation [religious activities as opposed to a vital relationship with God], and negative religious interactions [such as finding fault in church leadership and services].[5]

In short, trying to earn security and significance through our performance makes us self-absorbed instead of relishing the love God gives us, competitive instead of encouraging others, full of pride when we're doing well, and full of shame when we aren't, driven or passive (or alternating between the two), resentful of those who are getting ahead of us, prone to second-guess decisions and comments, terrified of being exposed, and always afraid of not measuring up.

We could make a long list of the effects of being driven by performance. Some of the most common include:

» We're always busy; in fact, we wear busyness as a badge of honor . . . or we give up in despair.

» We feel responsible for irresponsible people . . . or we avoid responsibility at all costs because we're sure we'll fail.

» We live with nagging self-doubt that we'll ever be good enough . . . which drives some and demoralizes others.

» We have to succeed, one-up, and win at all costs . . . or we give up and assume we'll always be inferior.

5 Christina L. Rush, Kevin S. Masters, Jannalee S. Wooldridge, et al, *Is Grace Amazing or Old Wind in a New Bottle? Psychometric Development of Perceptions and Experiences of Grace Scale* (San Diego: American Psychological Association, 2022), p. 10.

» We have to have our way . . . or we become so insecure that we never voice our own opinions.

» We're always thinking about the next thing we want to say in every conversation . . . either to gain the upper hand or to avoid looking foolish.

» We tell others who to be, what to do, and where to go, but we don't want any advice from them . . . or we don't believe we have anything to offer anyone.

» We live with a sense of superiority. We're not like "those people" . . . or we are "those people".

» We carefully create an in-group and an out-group . . . or we conclude we'll always be in the out-group.

» We live with a chronic level of anger and resentment . . . which can give us a lot of energy or sap our strength.

» We may brag about our wealth, our possessions, and our accomplishments, but when we're honest, we feel less than . . . or we're sure we'll never have anything to brag about.

» We lie to ourselves, to those we love, to others, and to God . . . or we grovel in self-pity and shame, telling ourselves the lie that our lives are hopeless and we're worthless.

As a leader of the Reformation, Luther's core beliefs were *sola gratis, sola fides, sola Scriptura, sola Christos*: grace alone, faith alone, scripture alone, Christ alone. He knew that changing the teaching (and the hearts) of the masses of people who had been taught conditional grace all their lives required discipline and determination. In his commentary on Galatians, he wrote about the need for church leaders to communicate grace: "It is also the principal article of all Christian doctrine, wherein the knowledge of all godliness consists. Most necessary it is, therefore, that we should know this article well, teach it unto others, and *beat it into their heads continually.*"[6] If that's what it takes . . .

To beat grace into our own heads, we need to camp out in some passages and truths that remind us of God's declaration to Jesus—and if we're in Him—to us too: "You are my beloved child in whom I am well pleased."

THINK ABOUT IT:

» *In our culture, how are temptations communicated to perform to meet our own needs, prove ourselves to others, and create an identity based on our wealth, intelligence, and strength? (Think of ads, commercials, songs, and other messages we hear.)*

» *Look at the list of the effects of trying to get security and significance from performance. Which of these is like looking in the mirror? Are there others not listed that affect you?*

6   Martin Luther, St. Paul's Epistle to the Galatians (Philadelphia: Smith, English & Co., 1860), p. 206.

CHAPTER 4

ENOUGH IS ENOUGH! . . . PAUL'S TAKE

IN THE SAME SPIRIT, LUTHER DEMONSTRATED CENTU-
ries later, Paul was blunt in his assessment of the church in Galatia.
After he left there, some men came from Jerusalem and taught
that Gentiles had to become Jewish proselytes and be circumcised
to become Christians. That meant they had to follow the Jewish
law. Paul didn't mince words even at the beginning of his letter.
. . . he was outraged:

> I am astonished that you are so quickly deserting him who
> called you in the grace of Christ and are turning to a different
> gospel—not that there is another one, but there are some who

trouble you and want to distort the gospel of Christ. But even if we or an angel from heaven should preach to you a gospel contrary to the one we preached to you, let him be accursed. As we have said before, so now I say again: If anyone is preaching to you a gospel contrary to the one you received, let him be accursed.—Galatians 1:6-9

Make no mistake: basing our identity on our performance is a "gospel contrary to the one you received."

When Peter went to Antioch, which was the first city in the Galatian region where Paul and Barnabas preached, he and Barnabas became convinced that the men from James were right. Before the men came, they were having fellowship with the Gentile believers as equals, but when the men taught a different gospel, Peter and Barnabas held themselves apart from the new believers. Peter was one of the most respected leaders of the early church, so other Jews followed his example. Paul describes the encounter:

"For before certain men came from James, [Peter] was eating with the Gentiles; but when they came he drew back and separated himself, fearing the circumcision party. And the rest of the Jews acted hypocritically along with him, so that even Barnabas was led astray by their hypocrisy. But when I saw that their conduct was not in step with the truth of the gospel, I said to Cephas before them all, 'If you, though a Jew, live like a Gentile and not like a Jew, how can you force the Gentiles to live like Jews?'"—Galatians 2:12-14

Let's make a few observations about this passage:
» No matter how high a leader might climb, it's possible to forget the message of the gospel of grace.

» Even Barnabas, who had been Paul's traveling companion and best friend, was fooled by the legalistic leaders.
» The gospel provides liberty and love; legalism produces fear and separation.
» The real issue wasn't the food or where they ate or anything else on the surface. Paul didn't rebuke Peter and Barnabas primarily for their behavior. He told them they weren't acting "in step with the truth of the gospel." They had forgotten grace, and it showed up in their superiority and exclusion of the Gentile believers.

But Paul wasn't finished. He drove the point home:

> We ourselves are Jews by birth and not Gentile sinners; yet we know that a person is not justified by works of the law but through faith in Jesus Christ, so we also have believed in Christ Jesus, in order to be justified by faith in Christ and not by works of the law, because by works of the law no one will be justified. —vs. 15-16

His comment about "Jews by birth" contrasting with "Gentile sinners" was probably a tongue-in-cheek jab at the Jewish leaders' air of superiority. He makes it clear that no one is made right with God (justified) by performance, but only and always by faith in Christ's finished work on the cross.

TRYING TO EARN OUR SECURITY AND SIGNIFICANCE THROUGH OUR PERFORMANCE ISN'T "HALF A BUBBLE" OFF FROM GRACE— IT'S THE OPPOSITE OF GRACE!

Paul explains, "For through the law I died to the law, so that I might live to God" (vs. 19). The law promises to save, but it can't. Its purpose is to show us our sin so we feel the need for a Savior. The law, then, played its part in Paul's life; failure to keep it drove him to the cross of Christ. Then, he makes a dramatic statement that explains another facet of what it means to be "in Christ": "I have been crucified with Christ. It is no longer I who live, but Christ who lives in me. And the life I now live in the flesh I live by faith in the Son of God, who loved me and gave himself for me" (vs. 20). If we are "in Christ," we were in Him when He died on the cross to pay the penalty we deserved to pay. And if we are "in Christ," He lives in us and through us, not because we deserve it, but because He freely gives himself to us. Paul sums up what he's been saying in this section of the letter: "I do not nullify the grace of God, for if righteousness were through the law, then Christ died for no purpose" (vs. 21). There it is. Trying to earn our security and significance through our performance isn't "half a bubble" off from grace—it's the opposite of grace!

WE NEED TO FLIP THE SCRIPT AND PUT GRACE ON VIDEO.

Just as Peter and Barnabas slid back into trusting in the law and performance to be acceptable to God, it's very easy for us to go back there too. In fact, as we've seen, it's the default mode of the human heart. Later in the same letter, Paul warns the Jewish and Gentile believers:

Formerly, when you did not know God, you were enslaved to those that by nature are not gods. But now that you have come to know God, or rather to be known by God, how can you turn back again to the weak and worthless elementary principles of the world, whose slaves you want to be once more?—Galatians 4:8-9

Enslaved? Really? Yes, really. It's a dark word that describes what happens to our souls when we forget grace and slip back to trust in our performance. How do slaves respond to demands? With fear and passivity or rage and defiance.

But the question is obvious: If the effects of trusting in our performance to earn security, love, significance, and esteem are so devastating, why do so many of us still insist on living under that dark cloud? And if the grace of God is so clearly and powerfully taught in the scriptures, why isn't it more attractive to us? We might come up with several different answers, but we'll settle on two: First, far too often, performance is on video, but grace is on audio. Images capture our attention far more than music playing in the background, and all around us, we see powerful videos of people striving to make it big. We need to flip the script and put grace on video.

Second, we experience a lot of satisfaction from our performance—misguided satisfaction, but satisfaction, nonetheless. Maybe a better word is pride. We see a contrast in Jesus's story of two lost sons. The younger son asked his father for his share of the inheritance, and because his dad was still alive, it was like saying, "Dad, I wish you were dead!" It was a horribly offensive demand. But his father gave him his share, which was a third of the estate. This son "squandered his property in reckless living"—wine, women, and song. He was destitute and found a job feeding pigs, which was the bottom of the barrel for a Jewish man. At his darkest moment, he came to his senses and determined to return home, but his offense was so terrible that he didn't expect to be reinstated as a son. He planned to ask his father if he could be one of the hired servants. Maybe then he could gradually pay back all he had taken. But as he approached the house, his father saw him, ran to him, and embraced and kissed him. The young man began his confession and his request to be hired, but the father interrupted:

> . . . Bring quickly the best robe, and put it on him, and put a ring on his hand, and shoes on his feet. And bring the fattened calf and kill it, and let us eat and celebrate. For this my son was dead, and is alive again; he was lost, and is found. And they began to celebrate. —Luke 15:22-24

This son had no expectation of being brought back into the family, but his father showered grace on him. But that's not the end of the story, and in fact, it may not be the most important part of the story. Jesus told this parable as he sat eating with some outcasts and a group of Pharisees stood around them grumbling about Jesus's love for those who were far away from God. The younger son represented the tax collectors and other sinners;— the older son represented the self-righteous Pharisees.

The older brother heard the celebration, and when he asked a servant what was going on, he was told that his wayward brother had come home, and his father was throwing an extravagant party for him. The older brother was furious and refused to join the party. His father went out into the field to beg him to come and celebrate, but the older brother refused even his father's kindness. He resented his father for being so gracious to his brother.

That's how Pharisees treat grace, and that's how they treat people who delight in God's grace. Why don't they welcome it? Because grace doesn't value all the things we've done to prove ourselves and earn approval—from God or other people. There's no extra credit for long hours and sweat in hard work. The older brother and the Pharisees believed they deserved God's blessings because they were good enough, they'd followed the law well enough, and they certainly were better people than the younger brother, the hated tax collectors, and the despised outcasts. Spiritual pride kept them, and it keeps us if we follow their example, locked into an identity that has everything to do with self-effort and nothing to do with God's limitless favor for undeserving people.

The younger son came to his senses and returned; he asked to be a servant, but instead, his father reinstated him as a treasured son. The older son was self-righteous and demanded to be treated like a valued son, but he acted like a servant earning his wage. When the younger son repented, he had nothing to lose. His life was a wreck, and he was desperate for another chance to even be near his loving father. But the older son's identity was tied up in being "the good son", "the hard-working, responsible son", and he couldn't open his angry fist to receive the grace his father offered. So, which son are you? Which son are we? If we spend our energies earning merit badges of personal discipline, attendance at church events, sacrificing, and serving, we'll go through the motions of being a child of God, but we'll miss his big, wide-open, loving heart.

Again, we're not saying that personal discipline, attendance at events, sacrifices, and serving are wrong. They're neutral. The issue with these things isn't *what* we're doing, but *why* we're doing them, and you'll never be able to sustain the what if you don't have the right why. These things can be expressions of a heart overflowing with gratitude and grace, or they can be a means to earn points. It's all about the heart.

To admit we've been older brothers, we need either to come to the end of ourselves, in all of our exhaustion and despair, and turn our hearts back to the Father, or we need to have the courage and humility to face our pride and self-righteousness, and come to the feast of grace. Or maybe both.

One of the most difficult, yet most liberating things we can do is stop playing the role of "the good Christian" and trying to impress others. Image management may have been our way of life for many years, but no longer. It's time to take off the mask.

Are you ready to say, "Enough is enough!"?

THINK ABOUT IT:

» *Does it encourage you or discourage you that even Peter and Barnabas slid away from the truth of the gospel and tried to live by rules again? Explain your answer.*

» *What are some of the emotional, relational, and spiritual effects of legalism, moralism, and the bent of human nature to prove ourselves?*

» *Who are you in the story of the two sons? Have you ever been the younger brother? The older brother?*

» *What does it look like to come to the end of your efforts to prove yourself? Have you been there? Are you there now? Why or why not?*

CHAPTER 5

TAKE OFF THE MASK!

MANY OF US FEEL LIKE WE'RE CONTESTANTS ON *THE Masked Singer* every day. The show premiered in 2019 with a simple but compelling premise: Contestants dress up head to toe and sing, while the panelists and viewing audience try to figure out their real identities. In each round, someone is eliminated and takes off the mask.[7] The first five seasons garnered the highest ratings about the eighteen to forty-nine-year-old demographic for programs not related to sports. The point is to "hide in plain sight", to be fully engaged without being fully known. The question—explicit and implicit—is always, "Who is that, really?"

---

7   *The Masked Singer*, Alex Rudzinski and Brad Duns, aired January 2, 2019, on Fox.

Like those contestants, most of us play the same game in our relationships. We can't and won't take our masks off unless we're convinced we're enough. Instead, we create elaborate "costumes" of our appearance, our intelligence, our wealth, and our power to fool the people in front of us . . . and everyone we value is a panelist, judging us and asking, "Who is that, really?"

When we wear masks, we're always on stage playing a role. We're not authentic, and we don't allow people to see us. We think we're doing well when people come to the conclusions we intended, but sooner or later, we feel empty and alone because those people are relating to a fictitious person, not the real one. It's terrifying to think that someone—even our spouse or close friends—would see behind the mask and know us for who we really are—because we can't take the risk of them scowling, laughing, or walking away.

We want to say from the beginning of this chapter that we're not advocating total transparency to anyone and everyone, but we're certainly pushing to find one trustworthy person to begin the process of becoming more fully known. If you can trust even a little, it will still seem like a huge risk to take a step into vulnerability. If the person responds with grace and understanding, you can take the next step, and the next. This is "a friend who sticks closer than a brother" (Proverbs 18:24). It's helpful to understand the difference between transparency and vulnerability. They may seem interchangeable, but they're distinct: Transparency is the volume and detail of the information you share; vulnerability is the meaning and emotion connected to that information. For instance, someone may say with very little expression, "I was verbally and emotionally abused by my father and abandoned by my mother when I was a child." That's transparency. But if this sharing of information is coupled with weeping or anger, and if the person then describes the impact of those wounds, that's vulnerability. How do you know if you can be truly vulnerable with someone? By being a little transparent with a fact and seeing the response. If the person is safe, you can then begin to connect meaning and emotions to that fact.

Of course, some people go far too deep far too quickly, and they risk being hurt, but others are so guarded that they refuse to take even the first small step of sharing a fact about themselves. Some of us, then, need to pull back and be more cautious, and others need to find one trustworthy person and take the first step.

WHEN WE LIVE ON STAGE, WE NATURALLY COMPARE OURSELVES TO OTHER ACTORS.

The fear of rejection was, for years, my (Travis's) chief motivation in relationships. I was afraid that if people really knew me, they wouldn't like me, wouldn't love me, and wouldn't want to be around me. I was sure the real me wasn't enough, so I didn't want anyone to know the real me. In every conversation, every meeting, and every encounter, I wore the mask of a wise, secure, and loving leader. That's how I wanted people to think of me . . . and for the most part, they did. But they didn't really know me. For years, I couldn't even imagine having one person who was safe enough for me to take the first step of transparency and the subsequent steps of vulnerability. And then I met Ben. Our friendship was first based on his honesty about his struggles to base his identity and security on his performance, and when I saw him taking a risk with me, I mustered at least a smidgeon of courage to be honest with him. Each time we talked, we either took new steps into truth, meaning, and emotions, or we reinforced where we'd already walked.

When we live on stage, we naturally compare ourselves to other actors. We may not win the Oscar, but we at least want to be one of the nominees! Comparison can consume us, but realizing its power can lead to some practical if not temporary solutions. For instance, a stylish lady in a church always sat in the front. When someone asked her about it, she explained, "If I sit in the middle or the back, I spend the entire service looking at the hairstyles of the women in front of me. If I want to focus on Jesus, I have to sit in the front."

We're not on every stage, but we're usually on the stage that's most important to us. Artists don't compare themselves to attorneys; they compare themselves to other artists: writers to writers, pastors to pastors, entrepreneurs to entrepreneurs, plumbers to plumbers. A successful attorney spent the first years of his practice consumed with winning a judgment that would impress other trial lawyers. When he achieved it, he felt wonderful, but only for a day or two. Then he set his sights on a much bigger goal. Each goal was a new, more refined, more powerful mask designed to impress his peers.

If we don't believe we're enough, we look for ways to give us some sense of connection, even if the connection isn't entirely personal. Some people, mostly men, easily wear the mask of an avid fan of their favorite sports team. Their sense of security and identity rises and falls with the won-loss record. They think about their team, argue with those who are fans of other teams, and live vicariously through the stars on their team. A study by the Department of Surgery at a major university hospital found that pride in a team can easily go too far, triggering riots after winning championships. On the other hand, "Those who feel a strong connection with the team tend to feel angry, upset, or depressed. After such a loss, fans can also suffer from symptoms of depression such as feeling tired, irritable, and hopeless. These feelings can also occur at the end of a season when fans are no longer able to look forward to watching their teams play."[8]

The masks we wear have two purposes: to hide deficiencies and project power, confidence, and strength:

Masks hide our fears.	Masks project false confidence.
Masks hide our insecurities.	Masks project strength.
Masks hide our anger and resentment.	Masks project superiority.
Masks hide our self-pity.	Masks project self-assurance.
Masks hide our secret sins.	Masks project having it all together.

We wear them because they work. In fact, they work really well . . . until they don't. We win the Oscar when people are impressed with us, or intimidated by us, or feel sorry for us, or need us. In all of these responses, we're in control of our image. Some of us wear masks in a desperate attempt to get people to love us, but others wear them as a power trip. One Christian leader growled, "I don't care if people love me. I want them to fear me."

8 "Living Vicariously Through Sports Teams: Is It Healthy?" Debra Wood, RN, Department of Surgery, NYULMC, https://froemkelab.med.nyu.edu/surgery/content?ChunkIID=14286

We continually add features to our masks to make them more presentable and to hide flaws. In each encounter, we're on stage again, and we hope the audience responds the way we planned. We feel stuck between who we really are and who we pretend to be . . . and that's a form of emotional and relational bondage.

EATING OF THE FORBIDDEN FRUIT OF GOOD IS JUST AS POISONOUS AS THE FORBIDDEN FRUIT OF EVIL.

Wearing a mask seems good, right, and reasonable. You could say that wearing one is part of our nature. In the account of creation, the Lord provided a perfect environment, perfect connection with Him, and a perfect purpose. And He commanded, "'You may surely eat of every tree of the garden, but of the tree of the knowledge of good and evil you shall not eat, for in the day that you eat of it you shall surely die'" (Genesis 2:16-17). Perfection, however, didn't last. In the next chapter, the serpent deceived Eve, and she ate from the forbidden tree. Adam followed her into disobedience. Our ancestors had a choice: to eat from the forbidden tree of good and evil or eat from the tree of life. Many people look at addicts, prostitutes, drug dealers, thieves, murderers, and others who engage in evil, and they claim, "I'm glad I'm not like them!" But many of these same people eat from the other fruit of the forbidden tree—the fruit of good actions, good behavior, good performance, and they don't realize it's the same tree! Like the two lost sons, we can wear the mask of a tough, "I don't care what you think" mask, but be dying inside, or we can wear the mask of manufactured goodness, and unless we "come to our senses," we assume we're perfectly in line with God. Eating of the forbidden fruit of good is just as poisonous as the forbidden fruit of evil. The only thing that satisfies is the tree of life. Wise King Solomon saw this truth: "There is a way that seems right to a man, but its end is the way to death" (Proverbs 14:12).

A pastor heard a message about how the gospel of grace invites us to take our masks off, and he commented to me (Ben):

> I live my life on a stage. I try to present myself to every person as a decent, competent, professional, kind person they can trust. I hear what you're saying, and you're right: I'm afraid to let people—anybody, actually—look behind my mask to see who I really am. To cope with the stress, I've been drinking . . . every day. How could I have gotten to that point? But I did. It's the only way I knew to pull it together for every meeting with people in our church. I don't know what life is like without wearing a mask, and I've been this way all my life.

I didn't give him a seminar on time management and anger control. I didn't recommend a book on leadership. I looked into his eyes and told him, "God knows the very worst about you, and He loves you still. You are fully known and fully loved. Your life might be chaotic, but the stress doesn't define you. In Christ, you're enough. In Christ, you overcome. In Christ, you're completely secure—no matter what."

When people read the passage about love in 1 Corinthians 13, they often end at verse seven and miss a remarkable truth in the subsequent verses. Paul explains that the genuine love he has just described operates in the context of vulnerability:

When I was a child, I spoke like a child, I thought like a child, I reasoned like a child. When I became a man, I gave up childish ways. For now we see in a mirror dimly, but then face to face. Now I know in part; then I shall know fully, even as I have been fully known.—vs. 11-12

When we try to project ourselves as someone we aren't, it's like playing hide-and-seek—a children's game—but for adults. Someday, the promise of the Bible is that those who believe will be with God face to face, but not now. Now we know God only in part, but when that blessed day comes, we'll know Him fully (here's the important part) "even as I have been fully known." No matter how much we're fooling other people with our hiding and projections, we don't fool God one bit. He knows us inside and out. Now. Not tomorrow, but today. King David marveled that God knew him so intimately:

O Lord, you have searched me and known me! You know when I sit down and when I rise up; you discern my thoughts from afar. You search out my path and my lying down and are acquainted with all my ways. Even before a word is on my tongue, behold, O Lord, you know it altogether. You hem me in, behind and before, and lay your hand upon me. Such knowledge is too wonderful for me; it is high; I cannot attain it.—Psalm 139:1-6

If someone knows everything about us but doesn't love us, it's terrifying. And if someone says they love us but don't really know us, it's superficial and less than meaningful. But God knows us far better than we know ourselves. He sees through the mask, under the mask, and behind the mask. Nothing is hidden from His sight. But we're safe in His loving arms. In John's first letter, he assures us, "See what kind of love the Father has given to us, that we should be called children of God; and so we are" (1 John 3:1). That's our present reality, and we have this strong hope: "Beloved, we are God's children now, and what we will be has not yet appeared; but we know that when he appears we shall be like him, because we shall see him as he is" (vs. 2).

THINK ABOUT IT:

» *What are some reasons people feel compelled to wear masks? What are the risks and rewards?*

» *What are some of the masks they (and we) wear? What are they trying to hide, and what are they trying to project?*

» *Complete this sentence: If people really knew me, they'd . . .*

» *How does it make you feel that God knows absolutely everything about you?*

CHAPTER 6

NO NEED FOR A MASK!

FOR YEARS, I (BEN) PLAYED THE GAME. I TRIED TO project an image of ultimate competence, but it was a charade. I lived with the nagging fear that people would find out who I really was, and they'd conclude I was a fraud. Thank God, that's changed. In the years since the gospel of grace has penetrated the strong defenses of my soul, I've been learning that I don't have to play that game. At all! I can rest in the Father's affection. I can relax knowing that I'm in His strong hands. I can have hope in every circumstance because the One who loves me to the stars is well aware of every flaw in the depths of my heart. For some people, this radical change in perspective happens in an instant. My path is longer, with more twists and turns, but the destination is the same: experiencing the love, goodness, kindness, and strength of God so much that I don't have to wear a mask any longer.

VICTORY ISN'T OUR ABILITY TO GIVE GOD A PERFECT LIFE; IT'S RECEIVING HIS PERFECT LOVE!

Do you live in fear of being uncovered, found wanting, and rejected? One of the most powerful and comprehensive passages about God's strong affection for us is in Paul's letter to the Romans:

> What then shall we say to these things? If God is for us, who can be against us? He who did not spare his own Son but gave him up for us all, how will he not also with him graciously give us all things? Who shall bring any charge against God's elect? It is God who justifies. Who is to condemn? Christ Jesus is the one who died—more than that, who was raised—who is at the right hand of God, who indeed is interceding for us. Who shall separate us from the love of Christ? Shall tribulation, or distress, or persecution, or famine, or nakedness, or danger, or sword? As it is written, For your sake we are being killed all the day long; we are regarded as sheep to be slaughtered. No, in all these things we are more than conquerors through him who loved us. For I am sure that neither death nor life, nor angels nor rulers, nor things present nor things to come, nor powers, nor height nor depth, nor anything else in all creation, will be able to separate us from the love of God in Christ Jesus our Lord. —Romans 8:31-39

Since Paul anticipates the reader's questions, we can read this beautiful passage like a dialogue. He had just described the wonder of our forgiveness and our adoption into God's family, and he asks, in effect, "What conclusion can we draw from this amazing grace?" If God gave us His precious Son, we can be confident that he will give us everything we need—including our complete security in His love. "Who brings us into the courtroom and threatens to charge us with being defective?" Not God. He has completely forgiven us and declared us righteous. "Who is a judge who condemns us as deficient?" Not Jesus. He paid the price for our deficiencies, proved it by rising from the grave, and now—all day every day—prays to the Father for our blessings. "Okay then, what's the limit of God's love?" There is no limit. No hardship, no difficulty, no attack, no angels nor demons, nothing in heaven or in hell can stop God from adoring us. That's the measure of His love and our security in Him.

> **WHETHER YOU WIN OR LOSE, SUCCEED OR FAIL, LOSE YOUR TEMPER WITH YOUR SPOUSE, OR EXERCISE MAGNIFICENT PATIENCE, THE LOVE OF JESUS ISN'T CONDITIONAL.**

Victory isn't our ability to give God a perfect life; it's receiving His perfect love! Good days or bad days—we're fully known and fully loved. Ups and downs, successes and failures, decisions that honor God and those that don't—God knows it all, and he's crazy about us!

Do you recall the story in John's gospel about the Samaritan woman Jesus met by Jacob's well? Jesus engaged her in a conversation about her checkered sexual past, and he assured her of His love and forgiveness. How did she respond? She left her water jar and told everyone who would listen, "Come, see a man who told me all that I ever did" (John 4:29). Notice what happened: The woman went to a well of water, where she found a limitless well of love in Jesus, and she became a well where others could draw plenty forgiveness and hope. Being fully known would have intensified her shame if she hadn't been convinced of Jesus's great love for her. It's the same with us.

God's love for you has nothing to do with your performance at work, at church, or at home. His affirmation is unwavering. Whether you win or lose, succeed or fail, lose your temper with your spouse, or exercise magnificent patience, the love of Jesus isn't conditional. He will never be ashamed of you or turn His back on you. He's the one who sees a glorious future for you even when you're at your worst.

Perhaps you can't relate to the points in this chapter because your mask is working so well that everyone is impressed with you. You're killing it at work, and you have your family under control. But someday . . . someday your mask will become frayed; it will slip, and you'll be uncovered. If you aren't sure that you're fully known and loved by God, that day will be a disaster. Don't be intoxicated by shallow or temporary wins of approval and success. For the unguarded heart, the only thing more dangerous than failure is success, because it tells us we can keep playing the game and winning. Affirmation based on performance is as addictive as cocaine or heroin. Our brain chemistry wants more and more of it to stay on the high. One of the problems, of course, is that the mask of a successful and competent Christian is just as powerful as any secular mask—and even more deceptive. It takes the Spirit of God and the honesty of a friend to show us we're playing that part.

Sometimes God delays our successes or allows roadblocks to cause us to stop and ask hard questions: "Why am I doing this?" "Who gets the credit?" "Who is the hero of my story?" God is more interested in the development of our hearts than our outward success. If He gives us success too soon, we may not learn life's most important lessons. . . . the ones we're addressing in this chapter. When our expectations are dashed, God isn't trying to hurt us; he's protecting us, refining us, and redirecting us so our identity is found only in Christ. If we keep wearing a mask, we may lurch from one person's approval to another and one achievement to another, but eventually, we'll burn out, we'll be disillusioned, or we'll finally realize our hearts have been hooked up to the wrong source of love, joy, and strength.

As the truth of being fully known and fully loved begins to transform our hearts, we relax from the rat race of trying to prove ourselves, but paradoxically, we're more energized than ever to honor God in everything we think, say, and do. We want our lives to count, not for our fame but for His. We want Jesus to be the hero of our stories.

God loves you more than you'll ever know. That's why He sent His Son to pay the price we couldn't pay and give us the righteous standing we could never achieve. That's His stamp of approval on you. Welcome it. Embrace it. Believe it.

The voice of the enemy whispers or shouts that none of this is true, or maybe that it's true for other people but not for you. He will go to great lengths to erode the message of grace so that it doesn't liberate and inspire you. Learn to distinguish His voice from God's. Many people have been deeply encouraged by reciting gospel identity statements. You'll find fifty of them in the appendix, and you can download them at this site: bendailey. com/if-anyone-is-in-christ-he-is-a-new-creation/. But to whet your appetite, here are a few of them:

I am a saint, a trophy of Christ's victory.

I am a child of God, the apple of my Father's eye.

I am free from guilt and condemnation.

I am hidden in Christ and eternally secure.

I am my Beloved's, and He is mine.

I am God's treasure.

Does the idea of being fully known and fully loved scare the pants off you? If you're on the front end of this realization, it probably does. Hang in there. Someday, it won't scare you. You'll "come boldly to the throne of grace" because you know that's where you belong.

It's time to take off the mask.

THINK ABOUT IT:

» *Which of the passages in this chapter about God's love mean the most to you? Explain your answer.*

» *Who is one person you can trust enough to at least be transparent about one fact you haven't wanted people to know? Is there anyone with whom you can be genuinely vulnerable?*

» *How would your life be different if you were so secure in God's love that you didn't need to wear a mask any longer?*

PART 2

Enough

We use a question mark to ask some of the most important questions we'll ever ask. Our answers need to go beyond and beneath a reflexive "Yes, of course!" If God enables us to be honest with Him, we'll know the depth and height of His grace more than ever before.

CHAPTER 7

AM I REALLY LOVED?

GRACE SHOULDN'T BE A FOREIGN CONCEPT TO ANY believer, but sadly, it often is. In many Christian circles, grace has become mysteriously controversial. For those brought up in any sort of holiness tradition (like I, Travis, was), you're probably even more susceptible to the systemic suspicion that's aroused if the word grace is used more than two or three times in a single paragraph. Doing so in a sermon would produce a handful of raised eyebrows coupled with an instant, inward dialogue containing questions like: "Where's he going with this? This isn't one of those grace churches, is it? I wonder if he's one of those hyper-grace preachers. Is he talking about using grace as a license to sin?" (I honestly don't understand that last question. I've observed that people have been sinning for a long time without a license.)

About a year after my grace awakening, Tina and I sat on the couch scrolling through our phones when she spotted a Facebook post that caught her attention. She read it out loud, and it said something that, had we heard it a little over a year earlier probably would have provoked a verbal "Amen" followed by a few affirming emojis to express our support. The post sounded something like this: "We've had the grace movement. . . . now, when are we going to get back to a good old-fashioned holiness movement?" We both knew that the author of the post meant well, but his contrast of grace and holiness revealed what's true for many of us—he didn't really understand either one or how God designed them to work in our lives after the dawn of the New Covenant. It was obvious that, like many of us, the author of that Facebook post had never been taught that grace can't be watered down to a temporary, optional movement. According to scripture, grace is much more than that—it's the basis of a New Covenant that was established with the precious blood of Jesus. For the record, holiness isn't a movement either—it's the result of the finished work of Jesus on the cross and the glorious grace of God working in each of our lives, causing us to mature in our new identity in Christ (holy and righteous) once we've been born again.

THE GRACE OF GOD SETS YOU FREE TO BECOME THE VERSION OF YOU THAT JESUS CREATED YOU TO BE!

In some circles, trying to earn God's approval through strict holiness is still celebrated, but it's not something to celebrate. The Apostle Paul actually described a few of the attributes of Old Covenant ministry. He wrote that the Old Covenant is a ministry of the letter that kills, a ministry of death, a ministry of condemnation, and a ministry of fading glory (2 Corinthians 3:6-9). In his letter to the Galatians, Paul asks those who were abandoning the New Covenant life to go back to the Old Covenant concepts, "Who has bewitched you?" (Galatians 3:1) Not exactly the abundant life Jesus came to offer us! In his book, *Streams of Living Water: Celebrating the Great Traditions of Christian Faith*, author Richard Foster highlights the strengths and pitfalls of each of the six traditions of Christian faith, the holiness tradition being one of them.[9] The three warnings in the holiness stream are against legalism, perfectionism, and works-righteousness (trying to earn God's love, favor, and forgiveness through our own works). I read those words through tears—I could, to some degree, relate to all three in one way or another.

Many believers have compartmentalized grace to the salvation moment alone, and in doing so, we've lost the beautiful role of grace in the process of spiritual growth and development. This hesitation has produced a form of grace that's good enough to save us, but we're on our own to obey God enough to earn His affection. In fact, I've heard a lot of definitions of "cheap grace" that sound like they were taken directly out of the Old Covenant code and whose tone is full of shame and condemnation. I would like to offer you my own definition: Cheap grace is a legalistic version

---

9 Richard Foster, *Streams of Living Water: Celebrating the Great Traditions of Christian Faith* (New York: HarperOne, 2001), pp. 59f.

of grace that's strong enough to save you but too weak to keep you while you mature in your new identity in Christ, insulting the cost of the blood of Jesus and His finished work on the cross. In contrast, the Greek lexicon defines grace (*charis*) this way: ". . . the merciful kindness by which God, exerting His holy influence upon souls, turns them to Christ, keeps, strengthens, increases them in Christian faith, knowledge, affection, and kindles them to the exercise of the Christian virtues."[10]

Day by day we're going from glory to glory as Christ is being formed in us (2 Corinthians 3:18). His character and the fruit of the Spirit are becoming apparent as Jesus patiently and lovingly heals the brokenness in our hearts and helps us to see ourselves as the new creation we truly are—redeemed, holy, and righteous! His grace doesn't promote sin—it's what allows us finally to stop sinning! In the words of Paul, ". . . sin shall no longer be your master, because you are not under law, but under grace" (Romans 6:14, NIV). The grace of God sets you free to become the version of you that Jesus created you to be! God fully knows you and fully loves you. Despite your brokenness, He'll never leave you, forsake you, nor give up on you, because of His amazing grace. You've been saved by grace, and you are continually being transformed by grace.

Sometimes people ask me, "Travis, are you one of those New Covenant grace guys?"

I reply, "I sure am!" And sometimes I add, "And whether you know it or not, if you're a believer in Christ, you are too. There's nothing to be afraid of. Dive into grace!"

10 Bible Study Tools, "Charis," *New Testament Greek Lexicon-NAS*, accessed 10 October 2023, https://www.biblestudytools.com/lexicons/greek/nas/charis.html.

Is it really possible to be fully known and fully loved? Many of us sing the songs on Sunday morning, read the passages, and listen to messages about God's limitless love—and we believe it, but only to a certain extent. Perhaps we grew up in a family where love was conditional; we had to earn our place at the table. And some of us grew up in chaotic households where we never felt safe. For a few, suffering trauma as adults has shaken our world and we now assume life is unfair. . . . God is unfair. Make no mistake: we're desperate for love, and when there's not enough of it, we find substitutes, create defenses, and become convinced that we'll only feel loved if we meet others' expectations.

Our self-concept and our view of God are shaped to a large degree by our childhood experiences, primarily with our parents. This is the way God planned it. Of the institutions that bring meaning and order to our lives, the family is the primary set of relationships that is meant to reflect the love, wisdom, and strength of God. Children intuitively attach to their parents. This doesn't mean parents have to be perfect to raise emotionally, relationally, and spiritually healthy young adults, but it means we need "good enough" parents who provide enough stability and affection for young hearts to feel known and loved. Without that, children conclude that they're not only unloved . . . they're unlovable.

The truth is that virtually every marriage, every friendship, every working relationship, and every connection with people at church involves a measure of masking to manage our image. Those few who feel truly known and loved are rare. In fact, we're even more guarded around those closest to us because the risk of rejection is greater, and the pain of wounds goes deeper.

People who don't feel fully known and loved instinctively protect their hearts to keep from being hurt again, but the walls of protection become a prison to isolate them. Then, they're not only wounded but alone, which makes them easy targets for manipulation and more dashed hopes.

In less than "good enough" home environments, we internalize the pain, and we carry our misperceptions into our walks with God. In our faith, we often choose religious practices over genuine love:

» Religion moves away from others' pain, but love moves toward it.

» Religion says, "You got what you deserved," but love says, "I took what you deserved."

» Religion says, "I'll love you if . . .," but love says, "I love you, period."

» Religion says, "You're always at risk of being found less than," but love says, "Love never fails."

» Religion says, "You'd better not relax," but love says, "You're safe and adored."

» Religion says, "Fear of being found out drives action," but love says, "You're already found out and more loved than you can imagine."

We see this distinction clearly in Jesus' Parable of the Good Samaritan. An expert in the Mosaic law had just asked Jesus, "Teacher, what must I do to inherit eternal life?"

Jesus knew, of course, that the expert had studied and had His own answer, so he asked him, "What is written in the Law? How do you read it?"

The lawyer responded, "You shall love the Lord your God with all your heart and with all your soul and with all your strength and with all your mind, and your neighbor as yourself."

Jesus replied, "You have answered correctly; do this, and you will live" (Luke 10:25-28).

This is where things get interesting. The lawyer quickly scans his mental images about the people who might be considered "neighbors", and he wants to limit the term to acceptable people. He asks, "And who is my neighbor?" (vs. 29)

Jesus told a story of a man traveling from Jerusalem to Jericho, a route that was notorious for bandits. The man was attacked, stripped, beaten, robbed, and left for dead. If there was ever someone who needed some love, it was this guy! A priest happened to be walking by, and when he saw the man naked and lying on the road, he carefully avoided him by walking past on the other side of the road. A Levite, another line of priests, also saw the man and walked past him. They represent religion. The naked man's condition was, in a real sense, fully known, but the religious leaders didn't love him enough to help. But another traveler walked by, a Samaritan. This was a shocking point in the story because Jews despised Samaritans, but Jesus made him the hero of the story: He had compassion for the man, cared for his wounds, put him on his own donkey, and took him to an inn to recuperate. He paid the innkeeper for two more days of care and promised to pay more if it was needed. Jesus asked the lawyer, "Which of these three, do you think, proved to be a neighbor to the man who fell among the robbers?" (vs. 26)

The lawyer wouldn't even utter the word "Samaritan." He said only, "The one who showed mercy."

Jesus told him again, "You go, and do likewise" (vs. 37).

> ## ANY VERSION OF THE FATHER THAT DOESN'T HAVE ALL THE COMPASSION, KINDNESS, AND LOVE OF JESUS ISN'T AN ACCURATE PICTURE OF HIM.

It's remarkable that Jesus makes the Samaritan the hero of the story. It must have shaken the lawyer and the others who were listening. The religious leaders undoubtedly had reasons for why they didn't stop to help: they were busy, they didn't want to become ritually unclean, they didn't want to be delayed from serving God . . . but none of these reasons mattered to Jesus. The man was fully known by three men, but only one fully loved him.

I (Ben) heard about the love of God from the time I was a little boy, but a nagging sense of guilt and shame led me to conclude that God may love me, but He surely didn't like me. Yes, the Father sent Jesus to the cross to pay for my sins, but His motive was anger at me, not affection. So, I internalized the dualism of saying I believed in the love of God but living in fear that I couldn't ever do enough to please Him.

Any version of the Father that doesn't have all the compassion, kindness, and love of Jesus isn't an accurate picture of him. In Jesus's prayer before His arrest, He ended by praying:

> O righteous Father, even though the world does not know you, I know you, and these know that you have sent me. I made known to them your name, and I will continue to make it known, that

the love with which you have loved me may be in them, and I in them. —John 17:25-26

In this Scripture, "your name" is much more than a label like Bob or Maria. It signifies the person's character and role. So Jesus is saying, "I accurately represented you to them, Father, and I'll keep doing that by the Spirit."

A few decades later, the writer to the Hebrews made sure his readers understood that there is no variation in character between Jesus and the Father:

Long ago, at many times and in many ways, God spoke to our fathers by the prophets, but in these last days he has spoken to us by his Son, whom he appointed the heir of all things, through whom also he created the world. He is the radiance of the glory of God and the exact imprint of his nature, and he upholds the universe by the word of his power. After making purification for sins, he sat down at the right hand of the Majesty on high. —Hebrews 1:1-3

"The exact imprint of his nature"—this tells us that on the cross, Jesus wasn't the victim of a furious Father. We're all familiar with John 3:16: "For God so loved the world, that he gave His only Son, that whoever believes in him should not perish but have eternal life." But we need to keep reading. The next verse says, "For God did not send his Son into the world to condemn the world, but in order that the world might be saved through him." When Jesus was on the cross paying the penalty we deserved to pay, both Jesus and the Father were in perfect harmony in their motive to rescue you and me from sin, the very thing that was destroying us. It was the epitome of love.

THINK ABOUT IT:

» *How would you describe the impact of a stable, loving family, with "good enough" parents, on a person's self-concept, motivations, and image of God?*

» *How would you describe the impact on a child of a chaotic home? A home where at least one parent was emotionally or physically distant?*

» *Think through the Gospels. What are some ways Jesus accurately depicted the Father's character?*

CHAPTER 8

WHAT'S THE MEASURE OF LOVE?

IN THE OPENING OF JOHN'S GOSPEL, HE IDENTIFIES Jesus as "the Word"—the logos, the logic of God, the one who is the source of perfect sense. How do we know what's in someone's mind? By the words they speak. We know God's mind about us because Jesus is the Word God has spoken: "And the Word became flesh and dwelt among us, and we have seen his glory as of the only Son from the father, full of grace and truth" (John 1:14). These aren't pitted against each other, and they don't combine to make a whole. Jesus is full, 100 percent, of grace, and He's full, 100 percent, of truth. In fact, His truth is about grace, and

His grace is the truth. So . . . there it is: truth—we're fully known; and grace—we're fully loved. But John wasn't finished. He wrote, "For from [Jesus's] fullness we have all received grace upon grace" (vs. 16). The Father, Son, and Holy Spirit created a world where "heaven and earth meet"—the love of God is imparted, not to people who have proven to deserve it—but instead, to flawed, fallen human beings who desperately need His affection to give us stability, significance, and hope for the future.

> **WHO WE ARE IS DETERMINED BY OUR VIEW OF GOD, AND OUR VIEW OF GOD IS SHAPED BY OUR EARLIEST AND MOST IMPORTANT RELATIONSHIPS.**

What is your concept of God? It matters because the version you worship determines the person you become. Some of us are mean because we believe God is mean. Some of us hold grudges because we're sure God still holds a particular sin (or a bunch of them) against us. Some of us can't form good connections because we believe God keeps us at arm's length. But our perception of God may be just as deep and flawed but the opposite of what we think of Him. For instance, if we believe God is mean, we may try really hard to be kind, pouring ourselves out to help others and trusting even untrustworthy people. If we believe God holds a sin against us, we might become far too lenient with others who have hurt us. And if we believe God is distant, we may crave closeness and get into relationships that aren't good for us. You get the idea:

Who we are is determined by our view of God, and our view of God is shaped by our earliest and most important relationships.

Over the centuries, theologians and pastors have identified a number of common but misguided views of God. For instance:

» The senile grandfather God: He's nice, but He's disengaged. In fact, He doesn't have the capacity or desire to be engaged with us. We know He's there, but it doesn't really matter.

» The bully God: He delights to find fault, and He uses our every flaw to punish us. Intimidation—or just the threat of intimidation—is enough to keep us afraid and malleable.

» The accountant God: He keeps detailed records of every thought, word, and action, not to encourage us, but to focus on our sins and mistakes. We live with a sense that no matter how hard we try, we can never measure up.

» The bad cop God: He's hiding and watching to see if we'll cross the line. When we do (or even if we just think we do), He comes out of nowhere to condemn us.

» The mixed message God: He says He loves you, but you feel like He holds you close to keep you under His control, not to delight in you.

» The absent uncle God: We have good memories of God from long ago, but we don't connect with Him now.

» The vending machine God: We believe we can drop in our coins of obedience or giving and get the exact blessing we want. Sometimes we assume God's many blessings come only because we've done our part. We have no concept of a loving Father who delights in giving His children good gifts.

> » The therapist God: We believe God's highest goal is to make us happy, so we're frustrated, angry, and confused when things don't go well for us.
> » The cool dad God: We believe God doesn't care about our values and choices. He just wants us to "let it loose" and have a good time.

In the cross, we find three related pictures of God, and all of them are important if we want a clearer understanding of the true nature of God. The first is a teaching called *substitutionary atonement*. Many of us are familiar with this perspective: We deserved to pay the price for our sins, and we deserved eternal condemnation in hell, but Jesus took our place. He paid the debt we should have paid, and we receive the honor He deserves. It's "the great swap": our sins for His righteousness. Perhaps the best picture of substitution is found in Matthew's gospel. After Jesus was arrested in the Garden of Gethsemane, He was taken to the palace of Caiaphas, the high priest, for a trial before the Sanhedrin. There, He was falsely accused. He admitted that He was the Messiah, the Son of God, and then He stunned the religious leaders by claiming to be the divine Son of Man, a reference to the deity in Daniel's prophecy. He was accused of blasphemy and taken the next morning to the Roman governor to demand His execution. Pilate could tell the religious leaders were jealous of Jesus, so He tried to set Him free. It was the custom of the day for the governor to release one prisoner as a goodwill gesture to the Jews. He offered Jesus, but the leaders convinced the crowd to demand the release of Barabbas, a rebel and murderer. When Jesus was crucified, he was hung on the cross meant for Barabbas. He died in the place of a sinner, a criminal, a rebel, a killer. We are Barabbas. When Jesus was nailed to the cross, He took our place, suffering the judgment we deserved. The point is made even clearer because Barabbas means "Son of the Father". The real Son of the Father died in the place of another Son of the Father. We find the concept of substitution throughout the Bible, from the sacrificial system to the story of Abraham finding a ram in the bushes to sacrifice in the place of his son Isaac, to the teaching of Paul in his letters to the first congregations. If you read even a portion of the Bible, you can't miss it. But that's just one lens through which we can look at the cross.

Second, Jesus's death won the victory over sin, death, and evil. He is the conqueror, the ultimate overcomer, *Christus Victor*, who paradoxically, by His cruel death, brought life and peace to those who believe. A passage in Paul's letter to the Colossians blends the first two pictures of the cross: substitutionary atonement and victory over evil forces. He explained:

> And you, who were dead in your trespasses and the uncircumcision of your flesh, God made alive together with him, having forgiven us all our trespasses, by canceling the record of debt that stood against us with its legal demands. This he set aside, nailing it to the cross. He disarmed the rulers and authorities and put them to open shame, by triumphing over them in him.—Colossians 2:13-15

In the Roman world, those who couldn't pay their debts were put in prison, and above their door was nailed a record of all that was owed. Paul uses this idea to say that we were in prison because of our debt of sin, but Jesus nailed the record of our debts to His cross, where He paid for it in full. In that act of grace, all the power of evil, and the powers of evil, were disarmed. They can still shout at us, but they don't have power over us anymore. We're free because Jesus won the victory.

A third picture of the cross is the power of the love of God. We already looked at John 3:16: "For God so loved the world that he gave . . ." In Romans, Paul went into more detail about how the love of God led Jesus to the cross: ". . . but God shows His love for us in that while we were still sinners, Christ died for us" (Romans 5:8). We might say that substitutionary atonement is Paul's theme in the first three chapters of his letter to the Romans, and the love of God becomes his central theme in chapters five through eight, climaxing with a passage we saw earlier (but it never hurts to be reminded): "For I am sure that neither death nor life, nor angels nor rulers, nor things present nor things to come, nor powers, nor height nor depth, nor anything else in all creation, will be able to separate us from the love of God in Christ Jesus our Lord" (Romans 8:38-39). Love. That's God's motive behind the cross.

In *A Tale of Two Cities*, Charles Dickens gives us a glimpse into the heart of sacrificial love. The novel is set during the French Revolution, which saw vicious reprisals against political enemies, and the scenes shift between two cities, Paris and London. In the French capitol's Bastille prison, Charles Darnay has been sentenced to die under the blade of the guillotine. Sydney Carton looks much like Darnay. In an act of great love, he and some friends break into the prison, and Carton knocks out his friend Darnay. He takes his friend's clothes off and puts them on himself as his friends carry the unconscious Darnay out. Carton waits to die in Darnay's place. The next day, on the way to the guillotine, Carton is in a wagon with a woman who is also sentenced to death. She knows Darnay, and when she realizes the man in his clothes isn't him, she realizes what's happening. She asks, "Are you dying for him?"

Carton answers, "Yes, for him and his wife."

The woman is struck by Carton's enormous love for his friend. She tells him, "Stranger, it's going to be hard for me to die, but if I can hold the hand of someone so brave, so courageous, so loving as you, I can do it."[11]

You and I are Darnay. Jesus has stolen into the prison and taken our place. He suffered the sentence of death we deserve. But we are also the woman being carted to her execution. When we realize the magnitude of Jesus's love, we'll want to hold His hand for the rest of our lives. He is one "so brave, so courageous, so loving."

My (Travis's) family recently moved, and like most of us, we took some time getting everything in its place. We left our flatscreen television leaning against the wall in our bedroom. One morning as I was shaving, I heard a thump. A few seconds later, I heard our four-year-old, Savannah, say, "Mommy." Then another thump. This time, Savannah's voice was a little louder, "Mommy!" After a few more seconds, I heard a third thump. I realized Tina was in another part of the house, and she couldn't hear her name being called. I stepped out of the bathroom and turned the corner. Savannah had been playing in our bedroom and nudged the television so that it was about to fall, and she was stuck there trying to hold it up with her little hands. She knew she couldn't stay there all day, so she called out for her mother. When our eyes met, I could see the anxiety in her eyes. She had no idea how to get out of the mess she was in. She was either going to be stuck there, or she was going to drop the television and break it. I didn't say a word. I just

---

11   Charles Dickens, *A Tale of Two Cities* (London: Chapman & Hall, 1859).

reached down and held the television so she could let go. In those moments before I came around the corner, Savannah knew she was in trouble, but she didn't know how close her father was, and she didn't know how glad I was to help her. The situation was very perplexing and scary to her, but it was simple for me to rescue her from her dilemma. If she had known I was so close, she wouldn't have called to someone who was far away. She would have known I would respond to her pleas for help.

It was a beautiful moment in our relationship. I didn't say a word to Savannah about getting herself into a confusing predicament. She didn't even know how to explain what had happened, but it didn't matter to me. I was simply there for her.

Some of us will pray about anything . . . except the problems we've created by our poor choices. We're afraid God will blast us, or worse, that He'll turn His back in disgust. We may try our own brand of penance: doing a few extra things for God to make up for the mess we made or feeling bad enough long enough to prove that we're genuinely sorry. Neither of those coping strategies taps into the Father's loving heart, and both of them leave us feeling even more distant from him. C. S. Lewis wrote an inscription in a book he gave to his wife, "There are three images in my mind which I must continually forsake and replace by better ones: the false image of God, the false image of my neighbors, and the false image of myself."[12]

> ## OUR LOVE FOR GOD RISES AND FALLS, BUT HIS LOVE FOR US IS ROCK SOLID.

12 Walter Hooper, C. S. Lewis: A Complete Guide to His Life & Works, (New York, NY: HarperOne, 1998), p. 61.

Many of us have heard preachers use a passage in Revelation about the love of God as a club to beat people up. In the early chapters, John writes messages from Jesus to seven churches, one of which is Ephesus. God praises them for their tenacious faith, their endurance in hard times, and their rooting out of false teachers. Then He says, "But I have this against you, that you have abandoned the love you had at first" (Revelation 2:4). What is the "first love," the *protos agape*? Is it our love for God, and he's reminding us to come back and love Him like we did when our faith was new? That's how it's often preached, but if we scan the scriptures, we find that God is the initiator, not us. In his first letter, John makes his point very clear: "There is no fear in love, but perfect love casts out fear. For fear has to do with punishment, and whoever fears has not been perfected in love. We love because he first loved us" (1 John 4:18-19). God wants us to return (again and again and again) to the revelation of His love for us. If God's acceptance of us is based on our love for Him, we're in big trouble. Even though we're gloriously saved, we're still double exposures until we see Jesus face to face. Our love for God rises and falls, but His love for us is rock solid.

Does this seem like a small point? It's not at all. If the starting point is our love for God, we'll always have to prove ourselves. But if the starting point is God's love for us, then everything we are, everything we do, and everything we believe is a response to His great grace. We love God only to the degree that our hearts are flooded with the knowledge (*gnosis*) and experience (*epignosis*) of His love for us.

At this point, you might be thinking, *Man, the unconditional— in fact, the counter-conditional—love of God for me seems too good to be true!* We'd say, "It comes really close! That's what makes it so wonderful!" Paul was grasping for words when he tried to describe it in his second prayer in the letter to the Ephesians:

> . . . so that Christ may dwell in your hearts through faith—that you, being rooted and grounded in love, may have strength to comprehend with all the saints what is the breadth and length and height and depth, and to know the love of Christ that surpasses knowledge, that you may be filled with all the fullness of God. —Ephesians 3:17-19

In fact, we can't plumb these depths and reach these heights on our own. It takes the wonder-working power of the Holy Spirit to make God's love real to us. Paul concludes his prayer:

> Now to him who is able to do far more abundantly than all that we ask or think, according to the power at work within us, to him be glory in the church and in Christ Jesus throughout all generations, forever and ever. Amen. —vs. 20-21

Our bent is to try to earn love. That's the way the world operates, but it's not what happens in the kingdom of God. Love is a gift, only a gift. When we receive it and let it rummage around in our hearts, God shines His light on our defenses, our masks, our techniques of image management, as well as our fear of being found out, and our pride when we impress people. Why does He show us these things? To empty our hands of these substitutes so we can open our hearts to His great love. That's what God is about: a strong, wise, faithful love for us. Again, we look at Paul's letter to the Christians in Rome. He spends eleven chapters describing and illustrating God's grace, mercy, and love, and then he answers the intuitive question: So what? He writes:

> I appeal to you therefore, brothers, by the mercies of God, to present your bodies as a living sacrifice, holy and acceptable to God, which is your spiritual worship. Do not be conformed to this world, but be transformed by the renewal of your mind, that by testing you may discern what is the will of God, what is good and acceptable and perfect.—Romans 12:1-2

We're conformed to the world like wax in a mold . . . by outward pressure. But we're transformed from the inside out, by changing what we think and believe about God and the gospel. The will of God isn't just our obedience, it's obedience out of transformed, grateful, grace-drenched hearts. That's the impact of experiencing His love.

Yes, you're really loved!

THINK ABOUT IT:

» *Which of the false images of God do you see in some family and friends? Where do you think they got these concepts?*

» *Look again at the story from A Tale of Two Cities. How does it affect you to see yourself as Darnay? As the woman in the cart with Carton?*

» *What are some differences between intellectually knowing God loves you and experiencing His love?*

» *Do you have some fears, doubts, and pride in performance that is hindering your experience of God's great love for you? (We all do.) What are they? How does God's love overcome your resistance?*

CHAPTER 9

AM I REALLY ACCEPTED?

AS AN EXERCISE IN CONFESSION, BEN AND I (TRAVIS) want to admit that for many years, we heaped demands, with explicit or implicit condemnation, on the people who came to hear our preaching. We created cultures of judgment and shame, along with superiority and inferiority. Every Sunday, we dressed up our dysfunctions and communicated them with passionate zeal. We believed that was the message of the Bible. Actually, it's one of the messages—the message of the Pharisees. They, just like Ben and I, couldn't grasp the wonder of the grace Jesus taught and lived in every relationship. In the last several years as the grace of God has worked its way deeper into my soul, my message has changed, my demeanor has changed, and the lives of people listening have changed—all by the wonder-working power of the Spirit of God as people began to grasp the truth of God's great love, forgiveness, and acceptance.

Every person has experienced the highs of acceptance and the lows of rejection. We thirst for acceptance like a man in a desert craves a drink of water. This desire, this need, isn't a mistake, and it's not a flaw—it's the way God created us. Our greatest need is for His acceptance, but we also need the unconditional acceptance of a few people who represent God's heart to us. Actress Celeste Holm famously said, "We live by encouragement and we die without it—slowly, sadly, and angrily."[13] The unhealed pain of rejection festers into self-doubt, the condemning voice of our savage inner critic, a craving for affirmation, rampant insecurity, hiding from conflict because of fear or creating conflict to intimidate, a compulsion to fix broken people to prove we're valuable, and chronic anxiety about never being able to win the approval of those we respect. In our world, acceptance comes at a high price. To be accepted . . .

» You have to perform.
» You have to be first.
» You have to be the best.
» You have to impress.
» You can't show any flaws or failures.

When you live under this pressure, the fickle opinions of other people determine your acceptance, your value, and your security. To win acceptance, you have to play by their rules. If you don't, you suffer the consequences. When you think about the

---

13 Celeste Holm, "We live by encouragement and we die without it—slowly, sadly, and angrily," source, date, URL.

relationships you've had, you can probably see a compulsion to win acceptance: You signed up for classes you weren't interested in, you took jobs that sucked the life out of you, you got cozy with people who didn't really care about you, you stayed silent when you should have spoken up, and you either took great risks to win applause or you settled for a dull, limited life. Our desire to be accepted, to be wanted, to be the object of someone's desire, is one of the most powerful motivations in our lives—many would say it's number one . . . without a close second.

Most of us have at least some grasp of God's grace, but it's easy to drift back into trying to earn His acceptance. I (Ben) know because it happened to me. My mom and my dad (who was a pastor) were wonderful examples of love and grace, but when they suffered unfounded opposition from people in their church, I blamed God for not protecting them. For several years, I stayed away from God, but in the summer after I graduated from high school, God met me late one night. His love flooded my heart, and I delighted in His great kindness, forgiveness, and power. I could hardly believe God could love me so much. Years of fear and resentment melted away in the warmth of His love. But when I was in Bible college and listened to preachers in church, I heard two conflicting messages: God loves you unconditionally, but you'd better earn it! The negative one was bold and clear: "You'd better obey or else." "You aren't committed enough." "You'd better follow the example of faithful people in the Scriptures." "You're not praying enough, giving enough, or serving enough to please God." It's like grace let me in the door, but it ended at the threshold. From then on, it was works, obedience, and the grind of living under the threat of condemnation. I internalized these messages, and they shaped my identity. Grace evaporated into thin air. Now it was all up to me to prove that I was good enough to win God's smile . . . but it was never enough. I kept score against my friends at school, and then as a pastor against other pastors. Was I more committed than them, more successful, more popular, more skillful as a communicator and leader? When I failed, or I saw others succeed, I experienced a toxic blend of shame, envy, fear, and resentment . . . but I never identified those feelings and perceptions. I told people I was "fine," and I had "victory in Jesus." It took an awakening years later to restore grace to the center of my heart.[14]

Science teaches us that the pain of rejection travels down the same pathways in the brain as physical pain does. This means our body processes emotional pain in the same way it deals with a broken arm . . . but the soul doesn't heal as quickly as an arm, and we seldom provide as many resources for emotional wounds as physical pain. Unhealed rejection is like living with a swollen, infected, continually painful broken bone. Many of us can remember recovering from scrapes, cuts, and broken bones without any significant emotional memories, but flashbacks of moments of rejection take us back to the trauma and the intense emotions we felt then . . . and feel again. The memories stick in our minds, usually tucked away underneath the surface until something triggers them again, and then we're flooded with unsettling emotions again. Unhealed hurts and ungrieved losses inevitably produce an undercurrent of fear, anxiety, and resentment. We replay the scenes over and over again, hoping that somehow, we

---

14 Ben Dailey, *Limitless: The Life You Were Mean to Live* (Arrows & Stones, 2022).

can make sense of them; but they still hurt, they still shame us, they still make us feel radically insecure.

WE DIDN'T EARN OUR ACCEPTANCE AS SONS AND DAUGHTERS. . . . IT'S A FREE GIFT.

The enemy delights in our predicament. We're in emotional quicksand—every struggle drives us deeper into despair, isolation, and desperation. His strategy of using flashbacks is designed to accomplish two goals: to convince us we're unlovable and to convince us we're unacceptable. These are two core needs of every human heart—love and acceptance. But many of us live with these nagging, powerful, internal messages: "You're not worthy of love." "You're not worthy of acceptance." When we believe these lies long enough (and it doesn't take that long!), they become the dominant theme of our lives, coloring every thought, interaction, and decision. Let's look at a few symptoms of insecurity.

1) We'll view the success of others as a threat to our reputation. We spend our time comparing and competing with others because we believe we're only valuable if we're one-up on them. We subtly, or not so subtly, whisper negative things about them because the easiest way for us to look good is to make them look bad.

2) We develop "the imposter syndrome", trying to impress people and hiding our flaws. We live with constant worry that we'll be exposed as a fraud, as defective, as unworthy.

3) We develop a codependent craving for affirmation. In the world of alcohol and drug recovery, family members are termed "codependent" because they're also affected by the substance and the addict's behavior. They devote their lives to trying to control the addict, desperate to "fix" the problem. In the same way, when we grow up and live in a condemning, graceless environment, many of us conclude that the best way to earn approval is to do everything in our power to fix others' problems and make them happy. In the deep recesses of our hearts, it makes perfect sense, but it makes us slaves to the smiles and frowns of the people around us.

4) We're afraid to fail. Failure . . . any failure . . . screams that we're defective, unworthy, and unacceptable. It tells us— and we're sure it tells everyone who's watching—that we're damaged goods.

5) We're fragile and easily hurt. If you hit a healthy person on the arm with a moderate blow, it may hurt for a few seconds, but it's no big deal. But try hitting someone whose arm is broken. The pain is intense! And lasting! A broken heart is like a broken arm: Those who walk around with chronically broken hearts are understandably defensive. Their chief goal in life is to keep anyone from touching the source of their pain, but of course, they live in the real world so that guarantee isn't possible.

6) We gravitate to safe people, but not the healthy kind of safe people. We feel more comfortable with those who are even more insecure and anxious than we are. These relationships make us feel superior, but they do nothing to resolve the nagging pain.

So, what's the solution to performance- and fear-based acceptance? A genuine experience of the grace of God in Jesus Christ. The opening verses of Paul's letter to the Ephesians put us on the right track from the outset. He wrote,

> Blessed be the God and Father of our Lord Jesus Christ, who has blessed us with every spiritual blessing in the heavenly places in Christ, just as He chose us in Him before the foundation of the world, that we should be holy and without blame before Him in love, having predestined us to adoption as sons by Jesus Christ to Himself, according to the good pleasure of His will, to the praise of the glory of His grace, by which He made us accepted in the Beloved. —Ephesians 1:3-6 (NKJV)

Does it say God blesses us "to the praise of our glorious performance"? No, it's to the praise of His glorious grace! How did this happen? He chose us to be His own, He declares us forgiven, holy, and blameless in His sight, and in love, He adopted us into His forever family. We didn't earn our acceptance as sons and daughters. . . . it's a free gift. We don't need to strive to attain it because we already have it! We're completely, absolutely, totally, unconditionally accepted. How? Because we're "in the Beloved." It's all because of Jesus. What freedom! What joy! What rest! What a relief!

THINK ABOUT IT:

» *How would you describe the price people pay to be accepted by others?*

» *Which of the symptoms of insecurity are issues for you?*

» *What are some reasons it's so easy to accept God's grace for our salvation but drift back into believing performance earns approval?*

CHAPTER 10
HOW FAR IN?

ALL OF US HAVE AN IMAGINARY SERIES OF DOORS, starting on the outside for everyone to see, and proceeding all the way into the deepest room in our souls. We hold the key to the locks on each door, and we determine how far we let anyone in— our spouse, our parents, our children, our friends, the people on our teams, our mentors, people we see occasionally, strangers . . . and God. The key to each door is trust. We let people in only as far as we perceive we can trust them, and our trust is (or should be) based on their proven trustworthiness. How much do they really know us? How do they respond to our flaws and failures? To what extent do we feel known and loved? Is our fragile identity safe in their hands? Is their opinion based on our good performance only? Or is it something richer, deeper . . . more solid?

Twice a voice came from heaven to proclaim Jesus's identity. At His baptism, a voice like thunder said, "This is my beloved Son, with whom I am well pleased" (Matthew 3:17), and again, at the transfiguration, the Father spoke the same words, but this time he added, "Listen to him" (Matthew 17:5). The first message came before Jesus performed any miracles, chose a disciple, or taught a single lesson. The second happened as He faced His impending death. The Father's affirmation that He was pleased with Jesus came from both ends of His ministry.

For years, I had heard pastors quote Ephesians 5:10: ". . . try to discern what is pleasing to the Lord." The implication was that the Lord is really hard to please, and I'd better shape up and work hard to do whatever it takes to make Him smile! The concept may not have been on the front burner of my mind all the time, but I lived under the subconscious pressure of it all day every day. But when I rediscovered grace, I realized that what pleases the Father is Jesus. There's nothing more pleasing to Him than His Son. Jesus didn't have to compete with the prophets for the Father's acceptance, and He wasn't burdened by the law. On the Mount of Transfiguration, the Father told the disciples, "Listen to Jesus." What is he saying to us? "Come to me, all who labor and are heavy laden, and I will give you rest. Take my yoke upon you, and learn from me, for I am gentle and lowly in heart, and you will find rest for your souls. For my yoke is easy, and my burden is light" (Matthew 11:28-30).

Who is eligible to come to him? The Pharisees had a rigid standard including all kinds of restrictions. Their rules disqualified people from approaching God because of behavior, gender, ethnicity, and health conditions. The "perfect storm" of rejection was someone who was sinful, foreign, a woman or had leprosy. But who did Jesus pursue with kindness and compassion?: sinners, Gentiles, women, lepers, and everyone else who was considered an outcast. He was making a theological point by His actions:

» The law excludes but grace includes.
» The law rejects but grace accepts.
» The law builds walls to keep people out, but grace builds bridges to bring people together.
» The law says, "You belong if", but grace says, "You belong because I love you".

Which realm do you want to live in? Do you feel unacceptable? Jesus says, "Come to me. Others may reject you, but I never will." His love embraced hated tax collectors, despised prostitutes, Romans, Samaritans, the mentally unstable, the demonically possessed, the physically handicapped, bleeding women, annoying children . . . and at least a couple of dead people! Jesus even welcomed a couple of Pharisees. Jesus accepted the unacceptable and loved the unlovable as a demonstration of the Father's gracious heart. We talk often about "receiving Christ", but a more important point is that He accepts us. And it's all about grace.

» In the eyes of the law, you were disqualified by your sin, but in the eyes of the Father, you've been qualified by grace.
» You were distant, but in Christ, you've been drawn close.
» You were dirty, but you've been washed clean.
» You were unacceptable, but he has accepted you in the Beloved.

Your status based on grace isn't just a ticket to get through the door; it's the foundation of your faith, the motivation to honor God, and the delight of your life. . . . it's everything! Grace takes you all the way into the throne room where you sit with Jesus at the right hand of the Father (Ephesians 2:6). In his letter to the Philippians, Paul explains that what God has begun in us He will complete: "And I am sure of this, that he who began a good work in you will bring it to completion at the day of Jesus Christ" (1:6). This means Jesus is the initiator in our life of faith, and He's the one who completes it. We can't add anything to grace by our obedience—we're not co-Saviors. That's what makes the gospel so wonderful. . . . Jesus has done it all!

> ## YOUR ACCEPTANCE ISN'T BASED ON WHAT YOU DO; IT'S BASED ON WHAT JESUS HAS ALREADY DONE.

Still, some people assume God's acceptance is like the conditional acceptance of the people around them. It's not! God isn't surprised that you have deep wounds and flaws. He's not going to put you in the corner or kick you out of the kingdom because you're messed up. Like we've said before: You're fully known *and* fully loved. No need for masks. No need to play games. No need to manage your image with God. Genuine acceptance is based on the knowledge of the other person. You can't truly accept someone unless you know them, and God knows everything about you. He knows everything you've ever done and everything you will ever do. He knows your darkest secrets and every skeleton in your closet. He knows your deepest hurts and your loftiest desires. And with His perfect knowledge, He delights to call you His own!

Many Christians treat God like He's their employer instead of their Father. An employer watches your performance and rewards you or gives you a negative review based on your attitude and actions. But even if a child is rebellious, and when a child is hurt, a loving father pours himself into that child to comfort, confirm, and direct. If you don't realize the scope of your acceptance by grace, you'll invest your energies desperately trying to earn something God has already given you. Your acceptance isn't based on what you do; it's based on what Jesus has already done. Yes, it's easy to assume God is your employer and live with the hope of promotion and the fear of being overlooked . . . or fired! You can become so busy earning approval that you can't slow down enough to hear God say, "You are my beloved child in whom I am well pleased! My love is limitless!" Some of us have a very high tolerance for spiritual and emotional dysfunction, so we live with it for years, decades, and sometimes our entire lives. But at points along the way, our gracious God taps us on the shoulder and invites us to follow Him into the revelation of our defenses, and then into the revelation that we're completely accepted by grace, so we don't need those defenses any longer. The questions are: Will we pay attention to the taps, and will we take His hand to follow him?

Four gospel truths can heal us from the pain of past rejection and the fear of being rejected again:

1) Discover that you're already fully accepted in Christ

Jesus understood the pain of rejection. He was ignored, criticized, falsely accused, and bitterly condemned . . . by the people He was dying to save! When Jesus was suffering on the cross, He screamed, "My God, my God, why have you forsaken me?" (Matthew 27:46) We come back to the truth of substitution: Jesus suffered rejection so we could be accepted. Jesus suffered dishonor so we could receive the honor of being called children of God. No one is more on your side than God. No one is more thrilled to know you than God. No one's love and acceptance are as deep and strong as God's. Until you grasp the wonder of God's acceptance, no amount of man-made acceptance can fill the gaping hole in your heart. Popularity is fickle. Possessions become obsolete. Power makes us use people instead of loving them. These make promises they can't deliver.

2) Discover that you're unconditionally loved

We looked at this truth already, but it fits here too. True love doesn't depend on the other person; it's a character quality, and God has it to the nth degree. In Deuteronomy, Moses explained to the people:

> For you are a people holy to the Lord your God. The Lord your God has chosen you to be a people for his treasured possession, out of all the peoples who are on the face of the earth. It was not because you were more in number than any other people that the Lord set his love on you and chose you, for you were the fewest of all peoples, but it is because the Lord loves you and is keeping the oath that he swore to your fathers, that the Lord has brought you out with a mighty hand and redeemed you from the house of slavery, from the hand of Pharaoh king of Egypt.—Deuteronomy 7:6-8

He loves you just because He loves you. It's not conditional at all. In fact, He considers you to be His treasure!

3) Engage in grieving and forgiving, which are essential in the healing process

We wish we could just snap our fingers and the painful memories would be gone, but that's not the way it works. We often think of grief only in relation to death, but we need to grieve every loss, including being abused or abandoned as children, ignored, or ridiculed as adults, suffering the rejection of divorce, and countless other losses. The grieving process isn't linear—we can't dictate when and how it will end. It's organic, ebbing and flowing, moving forward and backward for seemingly no reason, but sooner or later, the gaping wound is healed and only a scar remains. Forgiveness goes hand in hand with our grief. It's both a choice and a process. We enter into it with a courageous choice to not hold the wrong against the person who hurt us, but it takes time for the pain and bitterness to subside. Pastor and author Lewis Smedes wrote, "Forgiving does not erase the bitter past. A healed memory is not a deleted memory. Instead, forgiving what we cannot forget creates a new way to remember. We change the memory of our past into a hope for our future."[15] But many of us assume that forgiving someone means what they did was somehow acceptable. It's not. Smedes explains, "When we forgive evil we do not excuse it, we do not tolerate it, we do not smother it. We look the evil full in the face, call it what it is, let its horror shock and stun and enrage us, and only then do we forgive it."[16] (We'll address forgiveness in more detail in Chapter 22.)

15   Lewis Smedes, *The Art of Forgiving: When You Need to Forgive And Don't Know How* (New York: Ballantine Books, 1996), p. 171.

16   Lewis Smedes, *Forgive and Forget* (New York: Harper & Row, 1984), pp. 79-80.

4) Learn to accept yourself

This isn't an invitation to selfishness or to permanently camp out in the place of immature expressions of our spiritual identity (righteous and holy); it's an invitation to see yourself through God's eyes—as one who is the object of His delight, the source of His pleasure, the apple of His eye! When we can't accept ourselves—with all our faults and flaws—we continue to wear a mask and play the game to see if we can win acceptance and dodge rejection. We naturally treat ourselves the way we believe we've been treated. In other words, we absorb others' views of ourselves. We're not advocating arrogance, and we're not suggesting superiority. We're recommending that we let our guard down, at least a little at first, to let the unconditional acceptance of God envelop us. Then, we can relax. We can be ourselves. We can stop beating ourselves bloody for every perceived mistake. We can feel like kids of the king.

Experiencing God's radical acceptance revolutionizes our relationships. We no longer feel superior or inferior, just loved and treasured. We can now treat others the way God treats us. Paul said it simply, "Therefore welcome one another as Christ has welcomed you, for the glory of God" (Romans 15:7). How did Christ welcome you? With open arms and a heart full of love, with immense patience and sheer delight. If the acceptance of God overflows from your heart, how would your most important relationships be transformed?

Yes, you're really accepted!

THINK ABOUT IT:

» *What are some reasons it's significant that Jesus moved toward outcasts?*

» *How do past wounds shape our willingness to receive God's love and acceptance?*

» *How would you summarize each of the four gospel truths at the end of the chapter?*

» *How would the overflow of God's unconditional acceptance affect your relationships?*

CHAPTER 11

AM I REALLY A SON?

ONE OF THE MOST PRECIOUS AND BEAUTIFUL EVENTS in our world today is "Gotcha Day", the day parents go before a judge to officially adopt a child. In some states, the judge declares that the parents may, for some reason, choose to disinherit their natural children, but not their adopted child. The bond between adoptive parents and their chosen child is unbreakable. Similarly, one of the most precious and beautiful concepts in the scriptures is that the God of the universe, the one who was and is and is to come, has chosen to adopt us as His beloved children. The scriptures say that all of those who are "in Christ" are His sons.

If you're a woman, don't be offended by the word son. We're not making some kind of political statement. . . . the Bible is making a profound theological statement about the intrinsic value of each believer. In the Roman and Jewish world, women were second-class citizens. Husbands could divorce them for the most trivial complaint; women weren't allowed to give testimony in court because they were considered to be unreliable, and at home, they were considered little more than servants. Many Jewish men prayed each morning, "God, I thank you that I am not a Gentile, a slave, or a woman." The status of Roman wives was more like legalized prostitution. Their role was to be available for sex anytime the husband wanted and bear legitimate children.

Into this world stepped the Apostle Paul with a revolutionary concept: in Christ, women were valued as much as men, with the same status as the men. As we've seen, his letter to the believers in Galatia corrected their thinking about grace-based salvation instead of works-righteousness salvation, but that wasn't his only point. He explained that Jesus turned gender roles upside down:

> . . . for in Christ Jesus you are all sons of God, through faith. For as many of you as were baptized into Christ have put on Christ. There is neither Jew nor Greek, there is neither slave nor free, there is no male and female, for you are all one in Christ Jesus. And if you are Christ's, then you are Abraham's offspring, heirs according to promise. —Galatians 3:26-29

It's hard to say who would have been more shocked by this message—the men or the women. Suddenly, in Christ, the very roles Jewish men thanked God they didn't have to play became equals in the eyes of God. In Him, Jews and Greeks (meaning all Gentiles) are equal, slaves are on equal footing as those who are free, and women are as valued as men. And all of us have a seat at the table of the grand promise to Abraham—we're all heirs!

So ladies, if you're initially offended by being included in the category of "sons", you can have at least a little compassion for the men, who are called "the bride of Christ".

> **THE TRUTHS OF GOD'S LOVE, HIS ACCEPTANCE, AND OUR STATUS AS SONS AND HEIRS AREN'T THREE DISTINCT CONCEPTS . . . THEY INTERLOCK AND OVERLAP.**

The challenge to grasp the concept of sonship isn't just for women; men find it just as hard, not because of gender but because of inferiority. The truths of God's love, His acceptance, and our status as sons and heirs aren't three distinct concepts . . . they interlock and overlap. They are looking at our status before God from three different angles.

Some might respond to our emphasis on inferiority and announce, "That's only one side of the problem. Superiority is the issue of my spouse, my ex, my child, my boss." We get it. In most cases, superiority is the way someone compensates for their deep feelings of inferiority. Yes, there are some personality disorders, such as narcissism and sociopathology, where a person truly believes he or she is superior—and you may be living with one!—but most of us use superiority as a cover for believing we're less valuable and less worthy than those around us.

The festering belief that we're "less than" isn't a passing idea for many of us. It's our most deeply rooted, most powerful, most pervasive "truth" that determines everything about us. No matter how hard we try, we believe we'll always fall short and be the object of ridicule or mocking laughter, solidifying our view that we're tragically defective. For some of us, this self-perception haunts us all day every day, but most of us find distractions from the heartache . . . until a failure, a snide comment or a hurtful memory reminds us of what we truly believe about ourselves.

The signs of chronic inferiority include:

Rampant comparison

We're always on stage, and we're always checking out the other actors. Are we getting as much applause as they are? Are we avoiding the harshest criticisms? We compare our appearance, our intelligence, our wealth, our possessions, our wit, our position, our spouses, our kids, our popularity, the number of likes we get, and virtually every other conceivable measurement to others. When we walk into a room, we scan it to see where we stand. Who is above us, and who is below us? Comparison and rest are inversely proportional—comparison keeps us on a treadmill trying to prove our value to anyone who's watching. Sometimes we win; most of the time we lose because we compare the best highlights of others against our normal life . . . or our worst days . . . so we usually come up short. To alleviate the pain of feeling deficient, we stay busy, even if it's doing things that don't really matter because honest reflection hurts too much.

Hypersensitive to criticism

People who are secure don't enjoy criticism, but they see it as an opportunity to grow. If it's valid, they take it to heart, see the blind spots, and make changes; if it's not, they rise to the challenge to love the person anyway, and perhaps set some boundaries. But most of us aren't that secure. Instead of patiently considering what the person says, we react. Psychologists call this "amygdala hijacking". The amygdala consists of two small glands in our brains near our temples. When we feel threatened, these glands react more quickly than the thinking process that happens in our prefrontal cortex—in other words, we react before we can think. In fact, amygdala hijacking is so powerful that it shuts down our ability to think. This process was helpful when our ancestors were surprised by sabertoothed tigers, but it serves us poorly in our day-to-day interactions. The point is that this reaction happens when we perceive a threat, and people who feel inferior see threats around them in virtually every interaction—especially with "that person" or "those people" who make them feel even more vulnerable. The initial reaction is fight or flight, but a secondary reaction a few seconds or minutes later is freeze or fawn. Fight is lashing out at the threat; flight is getting away as soon as possible; freeze is shutting down emotionally as a form of self-protection; and fawning is the attempt to placate the threat by being nice, doing what the person demands, and going above and beyond to be helpful.

Catastrophizing

We believe everyone is against us, nothing will go right, and calamity is unavoidable. We don't devote our time to problem-solving. Instead, our minds race with pictures of the worst possible scenarios. We imagine others' contempt and scorn, our isolation, and the unavoidable and tragic consequences of anything we try to do. The sky is falling!

Black and white thinking

In our insecurity, we look for certainty: we see people as all good or all bad, and we view situations as completely positive or disastrous. Secure people can live with ambiguity and are patient with the process of discovery, but people who feel inferior are knocked off balance by anything that isn't crystal clear.

Perfectionism

A commitment to excellence is one thing; perfectionism is something quite different. Perfectionists don't learn from failure. They use it as a club to beat themselves to a pulp for being inadequate. They devote inordinate energy to one or a few commitments to make sure they're exactly right, but they neglect other responsibilities, like rest and enjoyment. Perfection is based on the lie that doing things just right will finally achieve acclaim and security, and it may, but only until the next project or the next conversation, which always carries a high degree of risk of failure.

For decades, I (Travis) couldn't decide if I felt like I was on stage or in a fishbowl all the time. I knew people were watching me, and I lived under the crushing pressure to be everything they expected me to be. I may not be the most self-aware person on the planet, but I had enough insight to know that I failed to measure up over and over and over. Every failure was another nail in the coffin of my identity. Every time I second-guessed myself, it was like pouring acid on my skin—it hurt, and it wouldn't go away. I tried hard to project an appearance of having it all together, but

Tina and our kids didn't buy it. They saw beneath the curtain, and far too often, it wasn't pretty. I fought against my deep sense of inferiority with the one tool in my toolkit: trying even harder to perform to impress people. When others got praise and positions, I was jealous. When my competitors were criticized, I secretly rejoiced. Living this way wasn't a choice, or so it seemed—it was the only game in town. Then, between my new friendship with Ben and my grad school studies, I began to discover the power of the New Covenant and God's unmerited grace. I was able to heal—slowly, gradually, but genuinely—and let God become my source of love, identity, fulfillment, and acceptance, so I wasn't always looking for affirmation from the praise of people.

For me (Ben), comparison and competition colored every minute of every day. I was so preoccupied with my fragile, performance-based status that I couldn't relax, I couldn't let my guard down, and I couldn't afford for people to know the real me. My inferiority propelled actions of superiority; I wasn't going to waste time with people who couldn't contribute to my program of self-promotion. Every interaction, or the opportunity for interaction, was evaluated for what it could do for my reputation. I was a poser looking for a promotion. I heard leading pastors say that you become who you hang out with, so I refused to spend time with those I considered lower than me. But comparison and competition left me feeling very lonely. My despair was reinforced when I saw other pastors who were asked to speak on the biggest stages suddenly decide they were too far above me to spend time with me. It hurt, but grace changed everything. Ever since I began to grasp that in Christ, I'm a beloved son, my heart has changed, my relationships have changed, and my role in the lives of others has changed. Not long ago, I sat with a pastor who poured his heart out to me. I had tears in my eyes as we talked about God's magnificent love for us. I told him, "This conversation has meant more to me than any speaking invitation I've ever received." I never would have said that before the revolution of grace that God has produced in my life. . . . in fact, I never would have dreamed of saying it. Today, I get incredible joy from meeting with people to encourage them and resource them. I don't see anyone as above or below me. We're all equals at the Father's table. Oh, sometimes I get off track and veer toward the onramp of trying to overcome my inferiority complex with expressions of superiority, but thank God, it doesn't take long for Him to remind me to get back on the road of grace, love, and security.

THINK ABOUT IT:

» *How do you think the people in the churches of Galatia responded when they read Paul's statement: "There is neither Jew nor Greek, there is neither slave nor free, there is no male and female, for you are all one in Christ Jesus?"*

» *How would you define inferiority? What forms does it take in people's lives?*

» *Which of the signs of chronic inferiority can you relate to? Explain your answer.*

CHAPTER 12

HOW SECURE AM I?

OUR STATUS AS SONS OF THE KING IS THE ANTIDOTE to the poison of inferiority. If we are "in Christ", He imparts His status to us. Like Jesus, we *are* beloved by the Father, we are totally accepted, and we are granted a place at the table as sons.

Our status as sons is based on who we now are in Christ, not on who we were before. It doesn't matter if we have a drawer full of perfect attendance pins from Sunday school, and it doesn't matter if we used to be Mafia assassins—our status as sons depends only on grace. Paul wrote the Corinthians:

From now on, therefore, we regard no one according to the flesh. Even though we once regarded Christ according to the flesh, we regard him thus no longer. Therefore, if anyone is in Christ,

he is a new creation. The old has passed away; behold, the new
has come. —2 Corinthians 5:16-17

"Flesh" is used in several ways in the New Testament: it can
mean our actual bodies, it can mean our propensity to sin, and it
can mean our prior condition apart from Christ. Paul is saying,
"We don't look at our prior condition any longer. Things have
changed! We're new creations, not shackled by the sins and conditions of our past."

> ## WE STILL MAKE MISTAKES, BUT BECAUSE WE'RE SONS, OUR MISTAKES NO LONGER MAKE US.

The enemy of our souls often uses the pain and sins of our past
to keep our hearts from delighting in the truth that we're a new
creation. He whispers or shouts, "You weren't good enough, no
matter how hard you tried, and you'll never be good enough."
"Your best efforts fall horribly short." "You may be able to hide
your flaws from other people, but not me. I know, and I'll remind
you. You can count on that!" But those accusations are no longer
true because you're not trusting in your performance any longer!
You weren't enough, but Jesus is more than enough, and you're in
Him. In his letter to the Romans, Paul uses baptism to illustrate
the gospel truth that we died to our old life and have been raised
in Christ to something brand new:

Do you not know that all of us who have been baptized into Christ Jesus were baptized into his death? We were buried therefore with him by baptism into death, in order that, just as Christ was raised from the dead by the glory of the Father, we too might walk in newness of life. —Romans 6:3-4

So, inferiority is just a memory, not a reality. The Spirit of Jesus lives in and through us, and He's more than enough. When those poisonous thoughts come to mind, we can stand strong and refute them with the gospel truth that we're sons of the King. We still make mistakes, but because we're sons, our mistakes no longer make us. But know this—the fight is real. The enemy doesn't give up easily, so we need to fight with powerful weapons. Paul described the battle for our minds and hearts:

For though we walk in the flesh, we are not waging war according to the flesh. For the weapons of our warfare are not of the flesh but have divine power to destroy strongholds. We destroy arguments and every lofty opinion raised against the knowledge of God, and take every thought captive to obey Christ. —2 Corinthians 10:3-5

This is a description of siege warfare. For many of us, insecurity, inferiority, and self-condemnation are strongholds, but we aren't left without weapons. God has given us two things we desperately need: truth and a plan—the truth about Christ, the truth that we're accepted by grace and not performance, the truth that we're sons of the King, and the plan that every arrow shot by the enemy, which are memories of being less than, can be blocked by our shield of faith so they don't land and hurt us.

Our identity is very different from what the world offers. It doesn't come from what others call us, but from the one who claimed us as His own. By grace, we're forgiven and adopted. In the opening verses of Ephesians, Paul explains that the Holy Spirit, the one who whispers to our hearts to assure us we belong to God, puts a seal on our relationship with the Father. In those days, people put a seal on documents, and one was put on the tomb of Jesus, meant to assure protection and ownership. It didn't work for Jesus because the Roman seal was broken at the resurrection, but the Holy Spirit's seal assures us that we can never fall out of God's loving hands.

As sons, we have a role in expanding God's kingdom: "on earth as it is in heaven." This means we have delegated authority to be all God has called us to be and do all God has called us to do. God replaced our inferiority with royal authority.

Others may have rejected you, but Almighty God has lovingly welcomed you.

Others think of you as a sinner, but God calls you His saint.

Others may see you as a coward, but in Christ, you're a conqueror.

Others say you'll never be enough, but in Christ, you're more than enough.

Others say you're worthless, but on the cross, Jesus made the statement that you're worth His suffering, sacrifice, and death.

Others call you condemned, but God says you're claimed.

Many of us live every day in a courtroom. The prosecutor has leveled charges against us, and witnesses have testified that we're defective, unworthy, and unlovable. If we're honest, we know there's more than a little truth to what they say. But we have a defense attorney unlike any other. John wrote, "My little children, I am writing these things to you so that you may not sin. But if anyone does sin, we have an advocate [an attorney] with the

Father, Jesus Christ the righteous" (1 John 2:1). Jesus hears the charges and the testimony, and He steps up to say, "My client can't be found guilty because I've already paid the price, completed the sentence, and suffered the consequences." The verdict is in, and we're free. Paul used the courtroom analogy in Romans to show that under the law we were guilty, but Jesus paid the fine we couldn't pay, suffered the judgment that was rightfully ours, and died the death we deserved to die. We're no longer in the courtroom, and we no longer have to listen to the prosecutor's charges or the witness's damning testimony about us. We only need to look into the face of our defense attorney and hear Him say, "You're free. You're mine. You're loved. You're accepted. You're a child of the King."

Sadly, many believers live under the mistaken assumption that the jury is still out. They keep waiting for the verdict, anxious about what it might be. We know we're not under the judgment of the law, but we've adopted the law of Christian performance, which is really no different. It's the expectation of being "a good Christian", following another set of rules—actually, a higher and more demanding set of rules—because it requires performance not only of our behavior but the perfected purity of our hearts. We lived under condemnation before we were believers, and we still live under the threat of condemnation for not being good enough.

We're not on our own to live the Christian life. The Holy Spirit lives in us, and He gradually changes us from the inside out. He reminds us that the verdict is in, that God delights in us being His children, and that He will give us the power and wisdom to do all God has called us to do. Paul's mind and heart were saturated with the gospel of grace, and it gave him amazing security—not arrogance—but humble confidence that Christ had done for him what he couldn't do for himself. He also used the courtroom metaphor in his first letter to the Corinthians. They were a disorderly bunch—arguing, comparing, and competing—missing the heart of the gospel. But Paul spoke to those issues and more. One of the problems was that they compared Paul to Peter, Apollos, and other leaders in the early church, and they found Paul to be inferior. Under these not-so-subtle attacks, he wrote them:

> But with me it is a very small thing that I should be judged by you or by any human court. In fact, I do not even judge myself. For I am not aware of anything against myself, but I am not thereby acquitted. It is the Lord who judges me. Therefore do not pronounce judgment before the time, before the Lord comes, who will bring to light the things now hidden in darkness and will disclose the purposes of the heart. Then each one will receive his commendation from God. —1 Corinthians 4:3-5

He was saying, "Hey, I'm no longer in the courtroom, so it doesn't matter how you try to accuse me. And I don't even judge myself. I let God do it. It's His job, not yours and not mine. I already have the verdict about me, and I'll wait until Jesus's return for His judgment about you."

As we saw in Jesus's story of the two brothers, the younger brother foolishly demanded his share of the inheritance and wasted it, but his poverty caused him to realize the goodness of his father, so he returned home and experienced the joy of being a son again. We might say that his superiority and arrogance led to a disaster, which was his wake-up call. God may allow the consequences of our dumb decisions to change the trajectory of our lives, but even when we suffer colossal failure, we may wallow in our failure instead of following God's leading to return home to Him. The older brother felt superior to his wayward brother. After all, he hadn't offended his dad, and he hadn't wasted the family wealth. He had been faithful to work hard and do the right thing, but it wasn't from a heart of affection for his dad. He was proving to anyone who might notice that he was "the good son" who deserved respect. He was just as lost, but he didn't realize it.

The younger son assumed the magnitude of his sin disqualified him from being a son again, so he asked if he could be just a hired hand. His father was thrilled to have him back and welcomed him with open arms. The older son didn't understand the nature of being a beloved son. He believed his performance—his hard work and his dedication to not be like his brother—earned points with God. The younger son experienced love, forgiveness, acceptance, and sonship; the older son saw himself as an overlooked, overworked, underappreciated slave.

We see both of these characters in our churches every Sunday. Some of the people who sit in our pews, sing the songs, and respond to the message have done unspeakable things, but they've gladly received the welcome of the Father. Their inferiority led to an awakening, which produced humility, and finally restoration as beloved sons of God. But the hearts of those who feel superior because they haven't run off to "the far country" keep them from experiencing the love they could enjoy.

Which are you? Which do you want to be?

The Old Testament stresses the holiness of God and the distance the people needed to stay safe from His glory. We see a few encounters with the awesome God, such as Moses at the burning bush hiding in the cleft of the rock because he wasn't allowed to look at God's face, and the warning to the children of Israel not to set foot on Mt. Sinai—God's mountain—or they would be killed. But in the New Testament, though God is no less holy and mighty, He invites us into a relationship of closeness, vulnerability, honesty, and kindness. Author, professor, and theologian J. I. Packer wrote:

> The stress of the New Testament is not on the difficulty and danger of drawing near to the holy God, but on the boldness and confidence with which believers may approach Him. . . . In adoption, God takes us into His family and fellowship and establishes us as His children and heirs. Closeness, affection, and generosity are at the heart of the relationship. To be right with God the judge is a great thing, but to be loved and cared for by God the father is a greater. . . . He will constantly be showing us, in one way or another, more and more of His love, thereby increasing our love for Him continually. The prospect before the adopted sons of God is an eternity of love.[17]

Isn't that what your soul longs for? Of course, it is, or you wouldn't be reading this book. Amazingly, it's already yours. Bask in the Father's love.

Yes, you're really God's dearly beloved child!

---

17   J. I. Packer, *Knowing God* (Downers Grove, IL: Intervarsity Press, 1973), pp. 184, 187-188, 196.

THINK ABOUT IT:

» *What does it mean that we are "new creations"? In what way are we new?*

» *What does it mean to live like "the jury is still out, and the verdict is still in doubt"? Can you relate to that pressure and fear?*

» *Read Packer's quote again. What stands out to you? Ask God to make it real to your heart that you are His beloved son.*

PART 3

Enough

●●

We use the ellipsis to emphasize the need to continue the conversation about "enoughness" in our relationship with God and with others. The punctuation indicates something is missing, left out; something has been left unsaid; there's more to the story. And in our experience of grace, there's always more to learn and live.

CHAPTER 13

AFFIRMED, BUT . . .

WE READ THE SCRIPTURES ABOUT THE AFFIRMATIONS of God toward us—ones we've repeated many times so far and will continue to repeat because they're central to our walks with God—but somehow, they may not sink very far below the surface. Why is that?

> **WE COULDN'T GIVE WHAT WE DIDN'T POSSESS, BUT NOW WE POSSESS THE AFFIRMATION OF GOD, AND IT POSSESSES US!**

Children are sponges. They soak up the verbal and nonverbal messages, primarily of their parents but also of siblings, uncles, aunts, grandparents, teachers, and coaches. They don't need just a little affirmation; they need to be bathed in affectionate words, hugs, smiles, and every other way love can be communicated. In their earliest years, children are totally dependent on their parents for food, changing, and emotional warmth. When their needs are met, they learn to trust those who are bigger and stronger. To the extent they aren't met, children conclude the world isn't safe and strong people aren't safe. As kids begin to assert initiative, good parents let them fall and make mistakes without overreacting, and the children begin to develop confidence in their ability to cope with difficulties. To the extent parents are disengaged, disapproving, or overprotective, children internalize shame and self-doubt. The first few years set the course for the rest of a child's life. It's very difficult to overcome neglect, harsh treatment, or "helicopter" parenting as the child moves through childhood and becomes an adult, but the gospel can heal a broken heart.

Before we move on, let's look at some of the characteristics of people who didn't, at least to some degree, experience overwhelming affirmation as children. They . . .

» Feel uncomfortable with their emotions and either stuff them or vent them, or alternate between the two.

» Fail to understand the emotions, desires, and needs of others.

» Have unrealistic expectations of a spouse and friends.

» React emotionally instead of responding thoughtfully to disagreements and conflict.

» Keep their guard up to prevent being hurt again, but this limits the depth of their relationships.

» Are susceptible to anxiety, depression, and using substances to numb the pain.

» Choose a spouse and friends who treat them like their parents did because it feels familiar.

» Believe they need to create their own sense of safety and significance by dominating others, becoming weak and passive, or trying hard to please people.

When we become believers, all of this doesn't just go away. We bring all the baggage into our new relationship with God. In the first weeks and months, we may feel a wonderful sense of relief because we're truly loved for the first time in our lives, but sooner or later, God leads us back into the past to apply the gospel of grace to our deepest wounds. As our old hurts heal, they're replaced with God's kindness, compassion, and delight in us . . . and as this happens, we're able to affirm those around us instead of using them for our advancement or pleasure . . . or protecting ourselves from them. We couldn't give what we didn't possess, but now we possess the affirmation of God, and it possesses us! We really love people, and it shows! One writer commented, "Grace environments are where affirmations flow like confetti."

For this radical internal transformation to happen, we need to be convinced that God's tender affirmations are expressions of His true attitude toward us and that we're empowered to then lavish affirmation on others. However, if you've never received it, you don't have a deep well to draw from, but as we experience marvelous affirmation from God and our heart wounds heal, we have a new well, and we become ambassadors of healing.

One of the most powerful Bible study techniques is putting ourselves in the scenes of the gospels. We may identify with one of the disciples, someone in the crowd, or a person interacting with Jesus. Mark doesn't waste any time showing us the heart of Christ. In the first chapter, he takes us to an encounter with a leper. In that day, lepers were the dregs of society. We're not sure exactly what kind of skin disease was termed leprosy, but it was so bad that those who were sick with it were completely ostracized from the community. Just before this meeting, Jesus had been in Capernaum, the town in Galilee where Peter, Andrew, James, and John lived. He first healed Peter's mother-in-law, and then He healed other sick people and cast demons out of those who were possessed. Early the next morning, Jesus found a desolate place where He could pray. Peter and the other disciples looked for Him until they found Him. Peter said, "Everyone is looking for you" (Mark 1:37). What he meant was, "Hey, this healing thing is going great! We can't stop now. Come on back to town and heal more people."

But Jesus replied, "Let us go on to the next towns, that I may preach there also, for that is why I came out" (vs. 38). So, they hit the road.

Lepers weren't allowed in towns, so we can assume that the leper met Jesus somewhere on the road going into a community. Mark takes us to the moment: "And a leper came to him, imploring him, and kneeling said to him, 'If you will, you can make me clean'" (vs. 40).

Everyone else in Jewish society—from Pharisees and Sadducees to poor laborers and widows—stayed as far away from lepers as possible. In fact, lepers had to announce their presence if they were anywhere near other people. But Jesus wasn't like any of them. "Moved with pity, he stretched out his hand and touched him and said to him, 'I will; be clean.' And immediately the leprosy left him, and he was made clean" (vs. 41-42).

This short passage tells us volumes about Jesus. Touching the man should have made Jesus unclean, but instead, it made the leper clean. Who are you in the story? See yourself as the leper—an outcast among outcasts, scorned, mocked, and abandoned. Affirmed? Not in the slightest. When Jesus saw him, His heart broke, and he did the unthinkable: he reached out and touched the man's diseased skin. In the replay room in heaven, we'll get to see the look on Jesus's face . . . and the look on the leper's face when Jesus touched him. Then we'll see the sheer amazement and gratitude as he watched his skin become like a child's. (We'll also see the disciples' horror turn to wonder.)

In his essay, "The Emotional Life of Our Lord," B. B. Warfield studied all the passages in the gospels that mention or describe Jesus's emotions, and he concluded that one is mentioned more than all the others combined: His compassion.[18] We see compassion most clearly when it's a response to a need or a hurt, and the person is treated with kindness instead of contempt. But compassion isn't dispensed only occasionally; Jesus's heart of compassion colored every interaction with every person. That doesn't mean He never said hard truths to people, but He spoke the truth without despising them.

In these interactions, Jesus gave people three things: attention, affirmation, and an invitation. He had, literally, the weight of the world on His shoulders, but He was very patient with people, even those who couldn't understand Him and even those who didn't

---

18 Benjamin B. Warfield, "The Emotional Life of Our Lord," in *The Person and Work of Christ* (Philadelphia, PA: The Presbyterian and Reformed Publishing Company, 1989), www.monergism.com/thethreshold/articles/onsite/emotionallife.html.

yet believe Him. The gospels don't say that He looked people in the eyes, but that's what we can conclude when He touched the leper, put His fingers in the ears of a deaf man, and touched the hand of Jairus's daughter to raise her from the dead. We often assume we're too busy to give focused attention. Our agendas are too important, our needs are bigger than anyone else's, and our goals are more far-reaching . . . at least, that's the way we act. If our parents didn't give us much attention when we were kids, we can be sure of this, "God's eye is on us all the time. He never stops giving us His full attention."

Jesus gave affirmations. He didn't just say, "You're great!" He demonstrated that He valued them. Put yourself in the scene when Simon, a Pharisee, invited Jesus and His followers to have dinner in his home. As they reclined around the table, "a woman of the city, who was a sinner" barged in. We don't have to have a vivid imagination to know her background, and we don't need to wonder what the Pharisee was thinking. She brought an expensive alabaster flask of ointment, "and standing behind him at his feet, weeping, she began to wet his feet with her tears and wiped them with the hair of her head and kissed his feet and anointed them with the ointment" (Luke 7:38). The Pharisee was aghast! He grumbled, "If this man were a prophet, he would have known who and what sort of woman this is who is touching him, for she is a sinner" (vs. 39). Like the leper in Mark's account, this woman was considered unclean, and it would defile anyone who touched her. But that rule didn't bother Jesus, not even a little bit.

Jesus took this opportunity to communicate two truths: first, He welcomed the woman's extravagant offering of gratitude. We can assume He'd had an encounter with her earlier, and she was so amazed at His love, she couldn't wait to express her thankfulness and love for Him. And second, Jesus had a message for the Pharisee. He told a short parable with a loaded question: "A certain moneylender had two debtors. One owed five hundred denarii, and the other fifty. When they could not pay, he cancelled the debt of both. Now which of them will love him more?" (vs. 41-42)

The Pharisee answered, "The one, I suppose, for whom he cancelled the larger debt."

Jesus responded, "You have judged correctly." Then, he gave this woman the most amazing affirmation possible: he defended her in front of a powerful religious leader. He turned toward her but continued speaking to the Pharisee:

> Do you see this woman? I entered your house; you gave me no water for my feet, but she has wet my feet with her tears and wiped them with her hair. You gave me no kiss, but from the time I came in she has not ceased to kiss my feet. You did not anoint my head with oil, but she has anointed my feet with ointment. Therefore I tell you, her sins, which are many, are forgiven—for she loved much. But he who is forgiven little, loves little. —vs. 44-47

And He astounded the Pharisee by telling her, "Your sins are forgiven." The Pharisee considered the woman beyond God's help, but instead, she left the room having been deeply affirmed by Jesus when all the pressure was on Him to side with the Pharisee. Those in the room questioned Jesus's authority to forgive sins because only God can do that, and they weren't sure He was claiming that power . . . but that's exactly what He was doing! He told the woman, "Your faith has saved you; go in peace" (vs. 50).

Imagine being this woman. You have lived "in a far country" for a long time, with no hope of ever being accepted by "the right people". Suddenly, you meet Jesus, and He doesn't care who you are, what you've done, or where you've been. He looks past all that to express His love for you. And then, when you take the risk to display your appreciation, He affirms you in front of a hostile crowd (of one). He takes a great risk to show kindness, compassion, acceptance, and love. That's the nature of affirmation.

The third element is an invitation. In every encounter, Jesus invites people to believe, to trust Him to meet a need, or to follow Him. The look in His eyes and the strength of His reputation call people to Him, and He engages them with a question ("Do you want to be well?"), a summons ("Follow me."), or a call to a new lifestyle of grace-filled obedience ("Go and sin no more.").

If we think Jesus gravitated primarily to the middle class, we've misread the narratives. He didn't move toward those who had something to give back to Him. He engaged people who were down and out, but also, the up and coming like Nicodemus and Joseph of Arimathea. No one was beyond Christ's affection and His affirming words and gestures.

THINK ABOUT IT:

» *Do you agree or disagree with the description in the opening paragraphs of this chapter about the impact of parents on small children? Explain your answer.*

» *How would you describe the impact of your home life on your self-concept, your confidence, your ability to trust wisely, and your ability to love without strings attached?*
» *Imagine yourself as the leper in Mark 1 or the woman in Luke 7. What was it like for them to receive Jesus' compassion?*

CHAPTER 14

I CAN AFFIRM THEM, BUT . . .

SOME OF US ARE SKILLED AND EFFECTIVE IN COM-municating affirmation to those outside of our family and close friendships, but we don't give as much to those closest to us. What's that about? It may be because those close to us know us better and can tell when we're insincere. It could be that they've hurt us, and we withdraw from them emotionally and punish them with sarcasm and other passive-aggressive behavior. Or perhaps we've tried before, and when we didn't get a positive response, we gave up on them. Whatever the reason, proximity hasn't led to affective affirmation.

Our affirming words and gestures, though, must be genuine or they'll have a negative impact. A woman relayed the story of being emotionally abused by her mother and emotionally abandoned by her father. She grew up with an insatiable craving for love, and her unconscious strategy was to never make a mistake to prove she was acceptable and always give more of her time and energy than anyone expected so they would appreciate her. She lived every day with a debilitating fear of being found defective and thus couldn't shake the never-ending drive to please people. When she was in her forties, she began to experience the grace of God, and her heart began to heal. Gradually, she absorbed the truth of the gospel that in Christ she's enough. Her fear-driven perfectionism ratcheted down several notches, and she no longer felt compelled to please people. She was no longer a puppet on a string. She decided to have an honest conversation with her parents, to tell them she forgave them and let them apologize for how they'd treated her. However, only one of those goals proved to be attainable. She met with her parents, described her childhood pain and the impact they had on her, and asked each of her parents to forgive her for her resentment. She fully expected them to confess their sin of hurting her, but they insisted everything they had done was in love. She explained, "That's not love. At least, that's not what I now understand love to be." Still, they admitted no fault. In fact, they blamed any strain in their relationship on her. She walked out with yet another wound to grieve, forgive, and heal.

This woman had made such dramatic progress because God led her to a small group of women who, like her, had suffered childhood trauma and were experiencing God's grace together.

In their eyes, she saw the look of understanding and compassion she hadn't seen when she was a child. In their voices, she heard words of kindness and affirmation that were like beautiful music to someone whose hearing had just been restored. In their touch, she felt a loving connection that was entirely new to her. These women represented Jesus to her, and it made all the difference in the world.

God has made us relational beings. Americans may insist on being "rugged individualists", and we see a measure of individual courage in Paul and the other disciples, but we also see them connecting with others on a deeper level. They were spiritual entrepreneurs, but they always built great teams. Paul, especially, is sometimes seen as a go-it-alone, take-no-prisoners kind of guy. That image of him would have been a surprise to those who knew him best. He was in Ephesus for three years, the longest time he spent anywhere after he came back from visiting his hometown of Tarsus after he met Jesus. Years later, when he was on his way to Jerusalem to take an offering for famine relief from the churches in Greece and Asia Minor, he stopped at an island near Ephesus and asked the elders to meet with him. He encouraged them, warned them of the dangers to the church in their city, and then gave a long goodbye. Luke takes us there:

> And when he had said these things, he knelt down and prayed with them all. And there was much weeping on the part of all; they embraced Paul and kissed him, being sorrowful most of all because of the word he had spoken, that they would not see his face again. And they accompanied him to the ship. —Acts 20:36-38

The tough guy had a tender heart. His love for these men had touched them so deeply that they wept when he told them he would never see them again. His persistent and deep affirmation of them over the years that they were together transformed them. In the face of fierce opposition in the city, they led a faithful, loving body of believers. Paul had filled their emotional tanks, and they overflowed into the lives of others.

When I (Ben) was nineteen, I had a passion to serve God, but I had no idea how to do it. Pastor J. Don George had heard me preach, and for some reason, he saw potential in me. He affirmed God's calling on my life, and he brought me into the world of church leadership. Later, he proved to be a friend, mentor, and guide. In my book, *Collide*, I described his impact on me:

> "When we face life's deepest wounds, we shouldn't try to tackle them alone. During my difficulty with all the condemnation at our church, Don George was a constant friend and mentor. His perspective is, 'Like a fireman, you always run toward a fire, not away from it.' He wouldn't let me run and hide. He helped me face the problems head on. He often told me, 'Ben, there's the fire. Run toward it.'"[19]

My (Travis's) father in the faith, Mitchell Corder, believed in me when I didn't have the confidence to believe in myself. He invited me to a leadership conference at the Church of God in Cleveland, Tennessee, the oldest and most prestigious church in the denomination. In the middle of his address to the pastors, he asked me to come up on the stage with him. He introduced me and proclaimed what he saw in me in front of his peers. It was a pivotal moment in my life. Someone I respected affirmed me with

---

19 Ben Dailey, *Collide* (Avail is publishing this now, isn't that right?), p. 106.

sincerity and announced his vision for how God would use me. I'll never forget his impact on me.

Those who are making a difference in any shape or form almost certainly can point back to someone who believed in them—a parent, grandparent, uncle, aunt, teacher, coach, pastor, Sunday school teacher, employer, or someone else who gave focused attention, spoke words of affirmation, and gave an explicit or implicit invitation to open a door of opportunity.

MAN'S AFFIRMATION IS SUPPLEMENTAL, GOD'S IS TRANSFORMATIONAL.

A mutual friend told us that he leads a recovery group for abuse victims, men and women who were horribly treated for many years but found the courage to walk through the door to the group and begin the process of healing. They have vivid memories of the wounds and the people who hurt them, but when he asked, "Has anyone stepped into your life to love you, to affirm you, to draw you near?", many of them wept as they talked about an aunt or grandparent who loved them when it seemed no one else did or ever would. And now, in the group, they're finding more people who love them and see a better future for themselves. The wounds will take time to heal, but the compassion and understanding they find in the group provide the ointment they need.

Pastor Frederick Buechner described our compelling need for someone to notice us and care for us:

We hunger to be known and understood. We hunger to be loved. We hunger to be at peace inside our own skins. We hunger not just to be fed these things but, often without realizing it, we hunger to feed others these things because they too are starving for them. We hunger not just to be loved but to love, not just to be forgiven but to forgive, not just to be known and understood for all the good times and bad times that for better or for worse have made us who we are, but to know and understand each other to the same point of seeing that, in the last analysis, we all have the same good times, the same bad times, and that for that very reason there is no such thing in all the world as anyone who is really a stranger.[20]

Do you have enough affirmation to give you enough food to satisfy your emotional hunger?

Affirmation from people is important. It's the language of love that should be practiced daily. It can be healing, encouraging, and God-sent, but until I discover my "enoughness" through the affirmation of God the Father, people will never be able to give me enough to convince me I'm enough. Man's affirmation is supplemental, God's is transformational. That's not to say that God's affirmation doesn't come through people, because it often does, but knowing the difference between a kind compliment and a heaven-sent affirming word from the Father is the difference between being temporarily inspired or eternally impacted. If we never speak to our family's value, they'll start to wonder if they have any. Sometimes, pastors can be the worst at this. It's a bit of a paradox. Publicly, we can communicate proficiently, but we often struggle to communicate well privately. We can preach affirmation, hope, and love, but the same man who stood behind the pulpit in the morning can find himself sitting in silent

---

20 Frederick Buechner, *Secrets in the Dark: A Life in Sermons* (HarperCollins Publishers, Inc., 2007).

indifference in the afternoon. Healing is essential. Are you feeding those around you so that they're satisfied? That's what matters. That's what makes a difference.

No ifs, ands, or buts about it—the Father affirms that you're His.

THINK ABOUT IT:

» *Who has stepped into your life to affirm you, believe in you, and see a future for you? How was this affirmation communicated? How did you receive it?*

» *Do you agree or disagree that many of the most compassionate, insightful people were deeply wounded but experienced healing through the grace of God and the love of a few people? Explain your answer.*

» *Who needs your words and actions of affirmation today? What difference will it make?*

CHAPTER 15

FAMILY, BUT . . .

AFFIRMED PEOPLE AFFIRM PEOPLE BUT HURT PEOPLE hurt people. Loved people love people, but rejected people find ways to manipulate people so they feel powerful or safe . . . or both. As we saw, some of us give affirmation to people at work or in church, but when we walk through the door of our homes, we turn the valve off. This probably shows that our affirmation of others is performative; we're just putting on a show. Getting hurt is inevitable, but staying hurt is optional. God has put us in relationships—in this chapter, we'll look at how our sense of "enoughness" impacts our families, and in chapter seventeen, our connections with our friends, but we can only give open-handed and full-hearted love if we've experienced the transforming grace of God. As we've seen, unhealed wounds keep us stuck in painful, self-defeating cycles that cause us to believe we have to dominate, hide emotionally and perhaps physically, or do everything in our power to earn approval.

When I (Travis) walked down the aisle and said, "I do" to Tina, I was both thrilled and oblivious: thrilled that she said, "I do" back, but clueless that I was dragging the baggage from my failed first marriage into this new one. Old wounds of rejection were still gaping and raw, and it didn't take long for them to produce familiar patterns of fear, insecurity, and pride in my relationship with Tina. It wasn't her fault. I hadn't grieved and healed from my previous deep wounds. Tina tried to draw me close, but I pushed her away. To me, emotional intimacy was too much of a threat. (You can imagine how hurt and disappointed Tina was.)

Oh, my desire to be known and loved was just as great as anyone else, but it felt like too much of a risk, even with the person who had just pledged to love me through thick and thin. When her love for me prompted her to come close, my fear caused me to shut down emotionally. When she asked what was wrong, I insisted it was nothing. I didn't want my insecurities to be exposed, even to her. I quickly found out that if you don't deal with your pain, your pain eventually will deal with you. Over time, my impenetrable walls of fear and insecurity colored every interaction between us. My old wounds were creating new wounds in Tina.

Gradually, both of us became more fragile, more angry, and more reactionary. The frequency and intensity of our arguments increased, and our affection decreased. We were moving apart. I could see it in her eyes. I had been distant, and now Tina was shutting down emotionally to protect her heart and disconnecting from me. No matter how much or how often she tried to bring us back into the love we felt when we were dating, I wouldn't let her in. I was terrified that she would see me for who I really was . . . how utterly broken I was.

It wasn't fair to Tina. She was paying a high price for a problem she didn't create. The people who hurt me weren't around any longer, but the pain still lingered. No, it did more than linger—it devastated me and was poisoning my relationship with Tina . . . but that's the impact we have on others when our hurts remain unhealed. We push people away, and we shake our heads at opportunities because both require risks that we're not willing to take.

This trench warfare went on for months, but one day after one of my artillery barrages of self-pity and resentment, Tina stopped, looked at me, and announced, "I can't keep doing this, Travis. I love you, but I can't live this way." I was stunned. She was drawing a line in the sand, and she waited to see if I would cross it and come to her. For a long moment, I thought about what had to happen in the face of Tina's bold honesty. For the first time in our young marriage, I took a risk. I stopped pretending. I stopped leaning away from the pain and leaned into it.

BUT OF COURSE, TIME ALONE DOESN'T HEAL PAIN—IT INCUBATES IT.

At that moment, I opened my heart to be vulnerable with someone safe, and my healing journey began.

Today, twenty-three years later, we love each other more than ever, and we have six beautiful children. I've spent the last twenty years helping people and being surrounded by very gifted leaders, and I discovered time after time that my story isn't unique. Many people are skilled, creative, and dedicated, but they're like me—pains of the past had them stuck in the cycle of feeling hurt, being defensive, attacking, and withdrawing. Like me, they were missing the joy of being known and loved.

I met with a businessman who had achieved remarkable success in his career, but he told me, "Travis, something's wrong. Even with all of my achievements, I still feel empty. Well, no, that's not really accurate. Empty would be an improvement! I feel angry and depressed. I snap at people, especially my wife and kids, for the smallest thing, but then I'm AWOL from them because I don't have anything of myself to give them." I began talking about my experiences with unhealed hurts, and the lights came on in his eyes. He told me that he was a star at every job for two years, but then he was fired, or he quit. He always found a better job, but this pattern was repeated several times. Each time, he moved his family so he could take a new position at a different company, but after two years, they had to move again. A few months before our meeting, he discovered an unsettling fact: It took him two years to get settled in a new company and a new community, but at that crucial point, he intuitively sensed a threat. His response was to reject his boss and his peers before they could reject him. He told me it all started when his first job ended in a major conflict with his employer when he was blamed for something he didn't do. The pain of that wound, now twenty years later, had finally been identified. Now he was in the process of healing.

His coping method was the one most of us use: When we're deeply hurt, we don't have the resources or the courage (or both) to address it in a healthy way, so we bury it, assuming (or at least hoping) that "time heals all wounds". But of course, time alone doesn't heal pain—it incubates it. It allows the wound to fester, to become even more inflamed, until it affects everything in our lives . . . even when we insist it doesn't. Before long, the lingering hurt produces a wall of fear around our hearts—the fear of being hurt again, the fear of being exposed, and the fear of getting too close to anyone.

| OUR INSECURITY IS FERTILE SOIL FOR PRIDE. |

This fear is the incubator of insecurity. We believe we're not enough, and we'll never be enough. We orchestrate our interactions to minimize the risks, redefine trust, and avoid vulnerability at all costs. This is when we pose; we pretend to be someone we're not because we believe no one would truly care for us if they knew us. We choose the mask that gives us the most protection and gets us at least the semblance of love. And it works . . . most of the time. Unexpected setbacks and relational conflicts threaten to tear our masks off and expose us as frauds, so we battle hard to keep them in place.

Our insecurity is fertile soil for pride. No, not the good kind, like, "I'm proud of you for handling that difficult situation so well." And not the arrogant kind that says, "I'm better than you, loser!" This is the toxic kind of pride that says, "Nobody understands me. I'm on my own, and I'll never let anyone speak to my heart!" It's self-pity, which is still pride, but it's turned inside out. Look at the difference: Boasting demands, "I deserve to be admired and respected for all I've accomplished." But self-pity demands, "I deserve admiration and respect because I've suffered so much." In this sense, people who engage in self-pity want to be seen as "wounded heroes", not helpless victims.

So, in our efforts to protect ourselves from being exposed and hurt again, we unintentionally imprison our hearts. This is a huge problem because the most fundamental need of the human heart is to love and be loved. However, inside these walls and behind these cell bars, it's nearly impossible to love or be loved. In this condition, we live with fierce inner conflicts:

» We want intimacy, but we want to be safe from being exposed as defective.

» We pull people toward us, but only to a point. Then we push them away or reinforce our walls to keep them out.

» We long to be in relationships that are mutually warm and supportive, but we're sure that people would laugh, ridicule, or walk away if they looked behind our masks.

In our attempts to be safe, we become weak and vulnerable. Unresolved pain produces an inward voice constantly trying to convince us that we're not enough. Some people hide their vulnerability behind a confident, even demanding, exterior. In conflict, they "get big": they raise their voices, lean forward, state their demands and condemnation of anyone who disagrees, and glare and grimace at the other person. But many of us "get little": our voices quaver, we slink in our chairs, we look down, our minds become mush, we don't have an opinion on anything, and we try to get away as soon as possible.

THINK ABOUT IT:

» *What do you think it means to "lean into your pain"? Have you ever done that? If you have, what happened? If you haven't, is this a good time to start?*

» *What are some of the ways our family relationships are affected by burying our wounds of the past?*

» *Who is a safe person for you? How vulnerable are you with that person? What difference does it make?*

CHAPTER 16

FEELING STUCK, BUT . . .

THE CONFLICT CREATED BY OUR COPING STRATE-gies can go on for decades until we're put in the ground or Jesus returns, but there's another option: Conflict can actually be the catalyst for healing if we're willing to lean into it rather than away from it. That's the choice I had twenty-three years ago, and it's the choice I had dozens of times after it as I learned new ways of living, feeling, healing, and relating.

If we expose the wound to a safe person, the walls we've built can be torn down brick by brick, and we can step onto a new path of authenticity, grief over the losses, and letting others love us for who we really are.

Let me break this down into component parts:

Choose an honest moment

This is what Tina did for me—she spoke the hard truth even though I didn't want to hear it. That moment may come in the heat of an argument, but sometimes (quite often, actually) we're so emotionally fired up at that point that we can't listen to reason, and we can't receive love. It may be wise to let things simmer down, and then do some honest reflecting on what happened. If it's a pattern, if you begin to see that it's been going on for years, if you realize you've used intimidation, withdrawal, or codependent pleasing to try to make life work, you're having your honest moment.

Identify the source of your pain

Soldiers, first responders, and people who have experienced sudden trauma not only can remember the events, but they can't forget them! Post-traumatic stress resurfaces the memories again and again. But most of us have to work harder to identify the knife that cut us so deeply. If our wounds were caused by an abusive or distant parent when we were children, we may have to work hard to uncover specific memories, and sometimes all we find is the emotion created at the time. That's enough. We just need to be able to say, "No wonder I've had such problems relating to people and finding peace in my own heart!"

Face the pain

After you've identified the source, this is the hard part: doing the work to grieve the losses. After Tina called me out on my defense mechanisms that were ruining our marriage, I kept waiting for someone to come along and take responsibility for healing my heart, but I realized that person wasn't going to show up in a cape on a white horse and make everything okay. I had to take responsibility for my steps of progress.

When we've lived with heartache for years, we might think that "a geographical cure" is the answer. We decide that a new job, a new city, and new relationships will give us relief, but there's a problem: we take our broken hearts with us wherever we go.

Stuffing our painful emotions has a negative impact on physical health. We may suffer from high blood pressure, gastrointestinal problems, chronic headaches, and other, even more severe issues. We have to be real about our pain or our pain will be very real to us.

As we mentioned earlier, grieving our old wounds requires us to find someone who will walk that hard road with us; we need insights to see the damage and the way forward, and we need enough courage to keep going when things get hard . . . and they will get hard. But it's worth it. It wasn't until I leaned into my own pain that my old wounds began to heal. Through this process, I discovered that the best gift I could give Tina, our kids, and everyone else in my life isn't lavish presents . . . it was a healed, whole version of me.

Forgive those who offended you

We've addressed this once already, and we'll devote a whole chapter to it, but we need to mention it again here. Bitterness and resentment keep old wounds open and bleeding, making it impossible to heal. Offenses create debts; they owe us because they've done us wrong. If we carry the damage into every relationship, we try to extract payment of the debt from everyone around us. We have unrealistic expectations and fragile egos, a combination that never ends well!

FORGIVING THE PERSON WHO HURT YOU BEGINS WITH A FOCUS ON GOD'S FORGIVENESS OF YOU.

Forgiving those who have hurt us frees our souls from self-pity and resentment, and it has a positive impact on our physical well-being. Steven Stanford, the Chief of Surgery at the Cancer Treatment Centers of America, commented, "Unforgiveness is known to get and keep people sick."[21] The center now includes "forgiveness therapy" for their patients. Forgiving the person who hurt you begins with a focus on God's forgiveness of you. In his letter to the Colossians, Paul wrote, ". . . if one has a complaint against another, forgive each other; as the Lord has forgiven you, so you also must forgive" (Colossians 3:13). To the extent you experience God's forgiveness for your debts, you'll be able to forgive those who created debts by hurting you. This may prompt you to pray for the offender, and it may lead you to call them to say, "I forgive you." No matter how you handle it with that person, it certainly means that you release the person from the debt owed to you. But let's be clear: Forgiving the person doesn't mean what he did was okay, that it didn't hurt, or that he can do it again with impunity. That person is responsible, and it may be

---

21 A New Thing Ministries, "Unforgiveness & Open Doors," *A New Thing Ministries*, https://anewthingministries.com/unforgiveness-open-doors-2/.

wise to withhold trust until it is earned. Forgiveness is unilateral, but reconciliation takes both people choosing to move toward one another in understanding, patience, and forgiveness.

Find a safe person

After Tina and I had met with a counselor for several sessions, something totally unexpected happened: We met versions of each other we didn't know existed—a healed version that was able to give and receive love, uninhibited by fear, insecurity, and pride. These versions of us had been there all along, but they had been buried beneath all the layers of pain. We needed someone we could trust to help us uncover it, face it, grieve it, and heal it. Studies show that therapy works. Clients repeatedly reported that the benefits of counseling continued after the last session ended because they internalized new ways of thinking, believing, and relating.

All of us have blind spots, and those who have been deeply wounded have more than their share. After all, they've spent their lives telling themselves they're worthless, which isn't true, and they've crafted defenses to keep people from seeing the truth about them. We need a guide who knows how to help us traverse the rocky terrain of a broken heart, someone who can help us walk backward into the pain and forward into healing and hope. If we're serious about emotional health and better relationships, we need to invest in a good counselor. You and those you love are worth it.

Develop tenacious hope

You don't have to tell me that this road is a hard one. I know. I've been there. There were times that I felt overwhelmed by the pain. I felt helpless and hopeless, but my counselor and Tina continually reassured me that the process would be well worth the effort. And they were right. If you were picked up on the side of the road by EMS after a major accident with broken bones, you wouldn't expect a quick and easy recovery. You'd expect them to keep you alive until you got to the hospital, and then you'd be in the care of physicians who could perform surgery, set the broken bones, and stitch the cuts. Then the healing process takes time for bones to mend, cuts to heal, and bruises to stop hurting. During all of this, you cling to the hope that someday, sooner or later, you'll be okay again. That's a metaphor for the healing process of emotional wounds. Through it all, we can trust in the Great Physician to care for us. We can have strong hope because we have a good and powerful Healer.

If we don't believe we're enough, we almost certainly won't believe our children are enough. We'll lean on them to do well, but with the threat, "Don't embarrass me!" In our exasperation that our lives aren't under control, we'll try to control their moods and behaviors. That may work when they're very young, but as they grow, this is a very destructive strategy of parenting.

Children (and adult children) need to hear three messages from us: "I love you. I'm really proud of you. And you're really good at . . ." The first message is unconditional affection—no ifs, ands, or buts. The second recognizes character, integrity, and courage. The third identifies skills and talents and envisions a glorious future, not necessarily specific, but wonderful.

But we may need to undo some damage as we begin to change our messages. When my (Ben's) kids were little, my performance-driven mentality came out in my relationships with them. My messages weren't the three positive affirmations; instead, they were demands, "You'd better . . ." "You'd better not . . ." "Don't make me look bad." And if I was particularly exasperated, I'd say, "I can't believe you. . . !"

As God's grace began to capture my heart, I soon realized my messages to my kids were coming from an insecure, demanding heart. I had been treating them the way I believed God was treating me! I sat down with each of my kids to tell them what God was teaching me about grace, pointed out how I'd pressured them to perform, and asked them to forgive me. I told them, "I want to promise that I'll never do that again, but I'm just learning all this. I need your help. Any time you feel I'm pressuring or condemning you, will you tell me? I'd really appreciate it. It's the way I'll learn and grow . . . and it's the way I'll find out how to treat you with grace, love, and respect."

God's unconditional love sets us free from the urge to manage our family's image as a happy couple and their kids. When our hearts aren't filled and overflowing with God's grace, we have no choice but to manipulate our spouse and children to make them treat us the way we want to be treated and act in ways that make us look good. When we stop manipulating—or more accurately, when we confess that we've been manipulating and begin to treat them with respect—they may not believe us at first. They may think we're just using a different method to get under their skin and fool them. But if we're consistent in our love, they begin to relax, to trust, and to love us in return. That's the beauty of Jesus being enough for us and our families.

No buts—no matter how difficult your family situation may have been, God brings healing and hope.

THINK ABOUT IT:

» *Review the steps outlined in this chapter. What's your next step? When and how will you take it?*

» *What difference does it (or would it) make to give the messages to your children: "I love you. I'm really proud of you. And you're really good at . . ."?*

» *Why does someone who is trying to impart grace to his or her family need tenacious hope? What stumbling blocks might be found along the way?*

CHAPTER 17

FRIENDS, BUT . . .

WHEN WE READ THE GOSPELS, WE USUALLY OVERLOOK one of Jesus's biggest miracles: He had twelve friends after he was thirty!

Having true friends isn't optional. We're created for relationships, and we can't function properly without them. God, first; family, certainly; but also, real friendships. Author Donald Miller alludes to the importance of grace at the heart of trusting connections: "When you stop expecting people to be perfect, you can like them for who they are."[22] Author and speaker Leo Buscaglia observes, "A single rose can be my garden . . . a single friend, my world."[23] A study by the University of Oxford found that having a close friend increases happiness and fulfillment as much as

---

22 Donald Miller, *A Million Miles in a Thousand Years* (Nashville: Thomas Nelson, 2009), p. 206.
23 Leo Buscaglia, "A single rose can be my garden . . . a single friend, my world," *BrainyQuote*, https://www.brainyquote.com/quotes/leo_buscaglia_163836.

getting $150,000 in extra income![24] Yet research shows that true friendship is in decline across the board: For instance, today, people have half as many friends as they had three decades ago. For men, the friendship drought is particularly pronounced—half as many men receive the emotional support women receive: men's 20 percent to women's 40 percent.[25]

When we don't have grace-based friendships (even one), we believe we're always auditioning for a part in others' lives, and our "friends" are auditioning for a part in ours. When this happens:

» We're easily exhausted by all the effort to look acceptable.
» We're territorial: If someone is my friend, she can't be close to someone else.
» We resent those who have better, deeper, stronger friendships.
» We're jealous of them too.
» Our minds race with thoughts about what it takes to please that person and stay acceptable.
» Or our minds race with thoughts about something we said that elicited a frown.
» Or our minds race with thoughts about "that person" being everything to us (which is sometimes called enmeshment or relational codependency).
» We try to project that we're calm and cool, but we suffer from radical insecurity.
» We're tempted to do whatever it takes to win approval . . . and retain it.

24 Ruth Umoh, "Study: Have a Best Friend is Worth Over $150,000 in Extra Income," *CNBC Make It*, 4 May 2018, https://www.cnbc.com/2018/05/04/having-a-best-friend-is-worth-150000-in-extra-income.html.
25 Scott Galloway, "No Mercy/No Malice," ProGalloway, December 9, 2022, https://www.profgalloway.com/friends/.

When our relationships are based on performance, we try to hide that we're desperate for heart connections, but our fear activates strategies of self-protection and self-promotion, which creates a perpetual prison of isolation. I (Travis) know because I lived there for a long, long time. Even as a pastor, the grace of God hadn't penetrated deep enough into my heart to give me security and stability. When I looked into the eyes of people who might want to be my friend, my instinctive reaction was, "But am I enough? And is that person enough?"

The experience of grace transformed my friendships because it first transformed me. I rediscovered the joy of connecting . . . with no strings attached. I could be myself, take down my guard, and love people for who they are. The more deeply I experienced God's love, forgiveness, and acceptance, the more I could love, forgive, and accept others—and a few of them became close friends. For instance . . .

I've already described how I was so resistant to Ben's kind overtures of friendship. Our relationship today is a testimony to his persistent love. As my suspicion eroded, trust began to grow. Today, he's a true friend, one who is closer than a brother, someone who has earned my confidence and my vulnerability.

A few years ago, I (Ben) had to make some exceptionally difficult decisions about people at the church. I loved the people who were affected, and it tore me up. Kim, our kids, and some were really hurt. I told Travis what was going on. On a particular Sunday, I had to announce some difficult changes to the church, and I dreaded it. Travis got a flight from Atlanta, came to the service, and sat in the front row to support me. His presence was enough, but his words were even more powerful as he affirmed me and my calling during a very hard time at our church. We've preached each other's pastor's appreciation services. We don't just say we're committed to each other. We act on it. I've seen Travis's talent for developing leaders, and I've had him come to train our leaders, and he leans on me for advice. We're partners, comrades, and friends for life.

> **IT'S ONLY WHEN WE RECOGNIZE HOW CHRIST IS A FRIEND TO US, JUST AS WE ARE, THAT WE'RE ABLE TO IN TURN BE A GOOD FRIEND TO OTHERS.**

This begins to pattern our first experiences with grace, giving us the ability and desire to express grace to others to discover that they too are enough in Christ. This shouldn't come as a surprise to any reader. It's the theme of this book. And it's the theme of Jesus's life. Matthew tells us about a time when people, and especially the religious leaders, took issue with Jesus. They had been perplexed about John the Baptist, who was odd but played the role of Elijah, announcing the coming of the Messiah. But the people had been hesitant, cautious about believing John's message. Jesus told them they were like children calling to their friends, "We played the flute for you, and you did not dance; we sang a dirge, and you did not mourn." He was saying, "John and I have invited you into the feast of salvation, but you didn't want to join us. We warned you that judgment is coming, but you don't even care." Then things got personal. Jesus told them, "For John came neither eating nor drinking, and they say, 'He has a demon.' The Son of Man came eating and drinking, and they say, 'Look at him! A glutton and a drunkard, a friend of tax collectors and sinners!' Yet wisdom is justified by her deeds" (Matthew 11:17-19). Jesus broke convention by loving the unlovable. How? Because He was love itself. He didn't depict Himself as the judge of sinners, like the religious leaders, and He didn't say He lowered His standards and became like the sinners. He said He was their friend. And He still is. He is perfect and holy, but he moves into the lives of the broken and needy—which is everyone, in case you didn't know—and genuinely cares for them. In fact, one of the remarkable things we see in the gospels is that sinners, lepers, children, women, crippled people, and all other kinds of outcasts felt completely comfortable around him. Jesus accepted people before they changed, as they changed, and after they changed. The grace of the initial acceptance fueled the subsequent transformation. Genuine heart change—that's how people respond to someone (especially the ultimate Someone) who is a true friend. It's only when we recognize how Christ is a friend to us, just as we are, that we're able to in turn be a good friend to others.

The experience of grace frees us from the captivity of comparison. We compare because our natural human instinct is to see where we are in a pecking order. We want to be perceived as better and more than everyone else . . . or at least someone else! When we walk into a room, we intuitively check people out to see where we stand. When we hear success stories, we may applaud, but secretly, we try to find fault to bring the person down a notch or two; comparison is killing what could be great friendships.

What do we compare? Virtually anything and everything: clothes, weight, the title on the door, cars, houses, vacations, loyalty to teams, hair, complexion, shape, kids, intelligence, strength, the size of our churches, and on and on and on. Comparison is so pervasive that we can't imagine life without it. And today, social media allows us to carefully craft our public image. Some of us post pictures of a meal, a scene on vacation, a child's graduation, or something else to show the world (or at least those who follow us) that we're the epitome of cool. But we curate the pictures and captions. We don't show the fifty other pictures we didn't use because they weren't quite impressive enough. We see the cheerful children moments before they gripe and whine because one of them got a larger scoop of ice cream. We see the smiling, happy couple only moments after they were in a fierce argument about finances. They spent more time editing the video than patching up their frayed relationship. Behind the smiles, delicious meals, and happy times, people are broken, insecure, afraid, and struggling.

Our culture reinforces comparison. Virtually every commercial has two messages: one that says the product works, like a brand of toothpaste that will clean your teeth, and a second one that promises the product will make you wildly attractive and popular. That's the one the companies hope you'll believe because that's the one that taps into your deep desire for affirmation.

The grace of God shouts a very different message, in fact, the opposite one. We can stop comparing because Jesus isn't putting us on a pecking order to see if we're acceptable. And we don't have to fool him so he thinks we've got it all together. He doesn't love us *because* . . . he loves us *in spite of*, and that's what real friendship looks like. We love people as they are, not as we think they should be. When grace crowds out the compulsion to compare, we can stop pretending to be someone we're not. We reclaim our authenticity as God's beloved children, so we can relax . . . and we can truly love those who still feel they have to compare favorably to be acceptable. When I (Travis) became increasingly convinced that I was chosen by God before the foundation of the world and accepted solely by His grace, I traded the formula of "compare and copy others" to "trust and rest in Jesus." Comparison tells us our identity is always vulnerable; grace tells us our identity is as secure as the One who gives it to us. I was finally free to celebrate the people around me without hidden jealousy lurking in my heart stealing my sense of worth.

Grace also releases us from the compulsion to compete. Competition is the ugly younger stepsister of comparison—one immediately follows the other. Competition is driven by a "scarcity mindset"—the belief that no matter how smart we are, how much money we have, and how much power we hold, it's never enough. We need more. When I lived under the Old Covenant of performance, competition showed up in two ways: I hoarded what I had and refused to share with others, and I wanted what others had. I spent my time desperately trying to prove I was worthy of love and respect, so I could never let my guard down, especially around my competition.

GRACE SOLVES THE PROBLEM OF BASING OUR IDENTITY ON PERFORMANCE, SO COMPARISON AND COMPETITION NO LONGER CONSUME OUR HEARTS.

When we live on the treadmill of performance and competition, we try to be better than others instead of being in relationship with them. Not everybody is an adversary, but those who desperately pursue the same esteem see us as their competitors.

The first murder in the Bible was between brothers competing for a sense of worth. Cain and Abel brought sacrifices to God, but God only delighted in Abel's offering. Cain was furious that God preferred his brother's sacrifice, so, in rage, he killed Abel. If he'd been secure, he could have learned from Abel, but he competed with him, and it led to death for Abel and banishment for Cain.

When we compare and compete, we aren't true friends. We can't genuinely celebrate others' successes because their success is a threat to our advancement and popularity. We may actually want people to fail, or at least not succeed as much as we do. And we're stingy with compliments because they acknowledge the other person's success, which is a threat to our sense of security.

Discovering our identity in Christ releases us from a scarcity mindset and implants an abundance mindset. We realize God's love and grace are unlimited, more than abundant, so there's more than enough to go around: more favor, more opportunities, and more resources than we will ever need. Then, we speak the language of possibility and embrace an attitude of generosity. We don't need others to fail so we can feel superior. We get off that inferiority-superiority train. We're just as thrilled at another person's success as we would be if it were our own.

Grace solves the problem of basing our identity on performance, so comparison and competition no longer consume our hearts. When our identity is based on our activity, we're sure to live in misery. Then, to ease the pain of insecurity, we prescribe ourselves a dose of activity to feed our addiction to affirmation. To be sure, success in those activities quiets the barking dog of "not enough, not ever enough", at least for a while, but in this never-ending pursuit, we don't know who we are because we don't realize Whose we are. We live on a rollercoaster of highs and lows, always depending on circumstances to prove we're enough and the smiles of people to assure us they believe we're enough. But the doubt lingers that we ever will be, so the isolation of living a friendless life lives on. In the earlier referenced article on friendship, Scott Galloway notes:

> Studies have shown that loneliness impacts your well-being similar to smoking a pack of cigarettes a day and rivals alcohol and smoking as a primary cause of early death. Friendship in the United States is on the decline. Since 1990, the percentage of Americans with less than three close friends has doubled from 16 percent to 32 percent, and those with no close friends at all have increased from 3 percent to 12 percent. Put another way, 20 million Americans have begun smoking a pack a day.[26]

Comparison and competition are always chasing fulfillment, but it's always just out of reach and it's killing us, literally. They create the illusion that we'll finally be fulfilled one day when we achieve X, acquire Y, or rise to earn Z. We can't enjoy the gifts of God and the people He has put in our lives today. We miss out on the present joy because we're anticipating the illusion of a self-esteem home run tomorrow. Actor Jim Carrey commented that if everyone got everything they ever wanted, they would quickly see that it was never the answer to their problems. When we're that driven, who are our friends? Either those

---

26 Scott Galloway, "Friends."

beneath us who don't threaten us, or those above us who we aspire to become. But neither of these groups are treated as peers, co-equals, or true friends.

YOUR ACCEPTANCE AND WORTH ARE BASED ON WHAT CHRIST HAS DONE FOR YOU, NOT ON WHAT YOU'VE DONE FOR CHRIST.

Burnout is often the result of unbridled comparison and competition. Instead of living with a heart full of gratitude for God's grace and acceptance, holding realistic expectations instead of being driven to perform, we risk emotional and physical collapse by pushing harder and harder to earn affirmations and higher positions. For some, exhaustion comes on slowly, imperceptibly, like the proverbial "frog in a kettle" that doesn't realize the water is getting hotter and hotter until it reaches a boil. But others run hard and fast until they suffer a catastrophic break. Either way, recovery from burnout requires professional attention, time, and a radical change, not just in scheduling, but in the habits of the heart.

Grace speaks boldly and lovingly to those of us who have felt we could never slow down:

» "What you do isn't who you are."
» "The size of your house or car doesn't define your significance."
» "Your net worth doesn't dictate your self-worth."
» "The opinions of others don't determine your value."

Your acceptance and worth are based on what Christ has done for you, not on what you've done for Christ. These beliefs are the door to rich friendships. We don't need to play games; we don't spend our energies comparing and competing, and we don't need to guard ourselves against being "less than".

THINK ABOUT IT:

» *Among your circle of friends, what are the points of comparison, spoken or unspoken? What impact does comparing have on these relationships?*

» *Competition is the natural result of comparison. How does competing with others affect relationships? Is competing ever good, with positive results? What's the difference between the good kind and the toxic kind?*

» *How can a person tell that burnout is approaching? What are some steps to take to stop the progression?*

CHAPTER 18

NOT THEM, BUT . . .

WISE KING SOLOMON WROTE, "A MAN OF MANY COM-
panions may come to ruin, but there is a friend who sticks closer
than a brother" (Proverbs 18:24). Some of us have wonderfully
supportive, loving families who are our best friends throughout
our lives. That's such a treasured gift from God! But many of us
need to look outside our genetic connections to our spiritual
connections and find a friend or two who give and receive love
far more than any member of our families.

We can apply the truths from Paul's painful experience of "a
thorn in the flesh" to our need for trusted friends. He wrote:

. . . a thorn was given me in the flesh, a messenger of Satan to harass me, to keep me from becoming conceited. Three times I pleaded with the Lord about this, that it should leave me. But he said to me, My grace is sufficient for you, for my power is made perfect in weakness. Therefore I will boast all the more gladly of my weaknesses, so that the power of Christ may rest upon me. —2 Corinthians 12:7-9

Some have suggested his "thorn" was an eye disease or some other sickness, but we can take it at face value: it was "a messenger of Satan to harass" him. What is the message carried by the "messenger of Satan" in our lives? It can be many things, including insecurity. Some of us live with the enemy's voice in our heads every day that tells us, "You're not enough. You're 'less than'. You'll never measure up, no matter how hard you try. You'll never have friends because you're so flawed. And the friends you have now are playing the same game you are—it's all performance, masks, and posing. Get used to it. It'll never be any different." But God spoke to Paul's heart to assure him that God's grace is sufficient, and in fact, this very weakness, this deep and nagging pain, will actually become a source of great strength. How does this relate to friendships? As those of us who have felt so unworthy for so long and have kept people at arm's length to protect ourselves begin to experience the wonder of God's grace, we appreciate friendships more than those who haven't struggled with it. We have more insight into the ways people try so hard to impress others, and we have a deep appreciation for our new, secure identity that lets us be open and gracious to people. Trying to do enough to be enough is the thorn of insecurity—it prevents real relationships—but now, when we realize that in Christ we are enough, God's grace enables us to build and sustain authentic, meaningful, and life-giving friendships without the relational drain and drama of comparison and competition.

Will there be offenses and hurt feelings in real friendships? Of course, but friends don't let them poison the relationship. They address them honestly and apply the gospel of grace and the healing ointment of compassion to each other. Some friction is caused by differences in personality, and in most cases, these need to be overlooked. But instances of genuine harm from unkind words, flared anger, suspicion, and other new wounds need attention.

But sometimes, no matter how much we try to mend a rift, the strain remains. I (Ben) reached out to a man who didn't go to our church to build a friendship with him. For months, we met for lunches, we texted, and we got to know each other. I thought our relationship was on firm footing, but one night, I received a text that said, "I don't want you in my life anymore." I was stunned. I had no idea what had happened to make him turn on a dime. I texted back, but he had blocked my number. A few days later, I wrote him a letter, drove to his house, and put it on his door. In a few hours, he sent me another text, but this one was even harsher than before. At the end, he wrote, "Be here tomorrow. I'll talk. You listen."

When I told Kim about this exchange, she said, "Ben, I know how much people mean to you, and I know you really wanted to be friends with this man, but you need some boundaries. Nothing good will come of you meeting with him and inviting him to vent his anger at you."

In past decades, I don't think people handled conflict very well, but today, it appears that we're at a new low. A recent study reported that eighty-five percent of Americans said civility in our culture is worse than it was a decade ago.[27] Political division is especially harsh and seemingly intractable. Almost eight out of ten people said they want government leaders to compromise, but a Pew survey showed that nine out of ten of both Democrats and Republicans said the other side of the political divide presented "an existential threat" to Americans' way of life, creating "lasting harm" to the country. The authors observe, "And when the balance of support for these political parties is close enough for either to gain a near-term electoral advantage—as it has in the US for more than a quarter century—the competition becomes cutthroat and politics begins to feel zero-sum, where one side's gain is inherently the other's loss. Finding a common cause—even to fight a common enemy in the public health and economic threat posed by the coronavirus—has eluded us."[28]

> **WHEN TRUE FRIENDS DISAGREE, THEY DON'T REACT WITH HOSTILITY AND DEMAND COMPLIANCE WITH THEIR VIEWS. THEY LISTEN.**

In the last few years, political, racial, and ideological differences have gone beyond disagreement to outrage and defiance. Those who disagree with our views aren't just misguided; they're morally

27 Karen Sloan, "Civility is on the Decline, ABA Civics Poll Finds," *Reuters*, 28 April 2023, https://www.reuters.com/legal/government/civility-is-decline-aba-civics-poll-finds-2023-04-27/.
28 Michael Dimock and Richard Wike, "America is exceptional in the nature of its political divide," *Pew Research Center*, 13 November 2020, https://www.pewresearch.org/short-reads/2020/11/13/america-is-exceptional-in-the-nature-of-its-political-divide/.

repugnant, and any compromise is out of the question! Families and friendships have been torn apart. Sadly, many Christians are just as defiant and offensive. We aren't being salt and light to a world that needs a delicious flavor and clear vision of the compassion of Christ. In fact, those courageous leaders who point people to the example of Jesus and call us to love those who disagree with us are considered "weak" and "compromising", which are considered the worst flaws in an angry, polarized world.

If the gospel hasn't penetrated our hearts, disagreements produce two very different reactions, and we can ping pong between the two in seconds: fierce resentment and a victim mentality. We see disagreement as a threat, so we react to defend our point of view, and since that point of view is intimately tied up in our sense of identity, we attack and defend with all our might. But we can quickly slink into self-pity as victims: "Nobody understands me. Nobody cares. Nobody wants what I want. I'm all alone. Poor me." Rage and grievance . . . they are the currency of our culture.

When true friends disagree, they don't react with hostility and demand compliance with their views. They listen. With a genuine interest in understanding the person's point of view, they ask questions and listen. Their goal isn't to verbally bludgeon the person into submission but to understand their viewpoint so completely that they can explain the other person's point of view as well as they can after they've listened, asked, and listened again.

To find and develop great friends, we want to offer some suggestions:

Be observant

Notice how people relate. By this time in the book, you're probably learning to observe masks, posing, and manipulation . . . in yourself first but also in others.

Move slowly and carefully

Some people trust too much too soon, and they're easily hurt when things don't work out like they hoped. They need to be shrewder, take risks more carefully, and move slowly to build trust one step at a time. But others don't trust at all. They believe it's safer to stay apart. They need to be more courageous, take a risk to be a little more open with someone who has proven to be kind and considerate, and begin to build a relationship based on trust.

Practice progressive vetting

It's not wise to be "all or nothing" in the early stages of a relationship. Again, some of us are so desperate for a close friend that we jump in far too quickly and share TMI (too much information), but others don't jump at all. Friendships progress at a slow rate, one moment of vulnerability and affirmation is followed by another and another. Typically, we share concepts and see how they respond, then we share opinions, and then emotions. Many men never get beyond the concept stage of vulnerability. They need to be more real. But many women (we're stereotyping here, but stereotypes contain a measure of truth) can be a bit too quick to open up about their deepest emotions. They need to be a bit more guarded. When we take a risk to open our hearts a little more but it's not well-received, we need to slow down and see if that person is safe enough to continue. She may have just had a

bad day, or it may be a pattern we need to be aware of. When Ben
and I began our relationship, I started by lying to him. (Great
start, don't you think?) When he continued to move toward me,
my faulty antennae told me that he wanted something from me,
and that he was only being nice to manipulate me. When I spoke
up to voice this concern, he calmly and patiently explained that
this wasn't his objective in the least. We kept talking about our
shared interests in ministry strategy and the Bible, and as we got
to know each other, we began to explore matters of the heart—the
way the gospel frees us to live and love without manipulation or
fear. Our friendship grew step by step as each of us revealed a
little more about our hurts and shared a little more emotion, and
each time, the other responded with kindness, understanding,
and support. That's how we intuitively and progressively vet our
friends to see how deep we can go.

Whenever possible, deal with conflict and hurt as they happen.
Most of us have been trained to bury our hurts, but they don't
stay buried long. They infect the relationship, and the contagion
spreads to other relationships. When someone says something
that hurts our feelings, it's wise to say, "Wait a minute. Can we
talk about what you just said? I feel sad (or mad or afraid or whatever). I want a relationship of trust and respect, so we need to talk
about what just happened." Don't let the comment sit, soak, and
sour in your heart, clouding your thinking and consuming your
emotions. Some of us are pros at that! Deal with it quickly. At first,
we may not realize what happened until a day or two later, and
then we can address it. As we become more skilled and comfortable with our emotions, the time between the painful moment

and addressing it will get shorter and shorter, until we're able to address these times when they happen.

As we've seen in every chapter, grace-drenched friendships are always based on the wonder of God's love for us. When we're freed by the gospel from comparison and competition, we can be the kind of friends Jesus is to us. Missionary Amy Carmichael observed, "If I take offence easily; if I am content to continue in cold unfriendliness, though friendship be possible, then I know nothing of Calvary love."[29]

Find Jesus to be your best friend, and then let Him work in your relationships so you build lasting friendships based on love, respect, honesty, and kindness. It'll change your life and those around you.

No buts, true friends always let you in and never let you down.

THINK ABOUT IT:

» *How do you think Jesus feels about Christians today who voice as much resentment, demands, and grievance as unbelievers? When is anger justified? When is it a poor testimony?*

» *Think of two or three memorable commercials. What were the two promises in each one: what would the product actually do, and what would it do for the user's popularity and prestige?*

» *Which end of the spectrum (or the golden middle) do you find yourself: trusting too much too soon or unwilling to take any risk to give and receive love in a friendship? Explain your answer.*

---

29 Amy Carmichael, *If: What Do I Know of Calvary Love?* (For Washington:PA, CLC Publications, 2011), p. 34.

» *What are some ways to practice "progressive vetting"?*
» *How do you see Jesus's love, acceptance, and affirmation of you impacting the way you engage with friends?*

PART 4

Enough●

Periods are used at the end of declarative
sentences to identify the end of the idea. We
use a period in this section title to point to the
final reality that in Christ you are enough.

CHAPTER 19

EXPOSING WOUNDS FROM THE PAST.

WHEN I (TRAVIS) WAS ABOUT EIGHT YEARS OLD, I walked into the house one day to find my mother crying. I asked, "What's wrong, Mom?"

Through her tears, she told me, "Your dad is going to leave for a while."

I could tell this wasn't like he was going to the store and would be back, or he was going to work, or even that he was going on a short trip. He had a job with General Motors, but somehow, I knew his leaving our home wasn't connected to his career. My mother's weeping told me that this was something so serious that my little mind and heart could only begin to comprehend it.

My parents were separated for two years. As I overheard conversations in the early months after Dad's departure, I realized he'd had an affair. Sometime later, I overheard that he was pursuing a permanent relationship with the woman. It looked like the break would be permanent, and I had no idea what that would mean for my mother and me.

My Dad picked me up two weekends a month. I vividly recall him bringing me back to Mom's house on Sunday. I stood and waved as he drove away. I cried every time.

My parents weren't people of faith. We went to a Catholic church a few times a year, and we only went there because it was so convenient—right across the street. Later I realized that we went to church only after they'd had a huge, blowout argument, and they believed attending church for an hour would do something positive for them.

In the middle of those two years, I stood in the parking lot of a bowling alley and watched as a friend of my mother's tried to console her. Her friend's name was Mary. I'll never forget this moment; it was arguably the most pivotal moment in our lives. As tears streamed down my Mom's face, Mary looked at my Mom and said, "Judy, I don't have the answer for your marriage, but I know Someone who does." She shared the gospel with my mother, and she surrendered her life to Christ that night.

The following Sunday, we went with Mary to the Assemblies of God Church in our hometown of Saginaw, Michigan. These people had something I'd never seen before. They talked about having a real relationship with God, and it mattered to them. . . .

it mattered a lot. This was my introduction to a life of faith and the family of God.

To my surprise, a few months later, my father also trusted in Christ. He had come to our house to do some maintenance on our swimming pool and some yard work. Even though they were separated, he was committed to taking care of us. I was in the house, and when I looked outside, I saw my parents hugging. She had led him to Christ at that moment. God began to work in my father's life, and a year later, he pulled into our driveway with a truckload of furniture. The Holy Spirit had been working in his heart. He knew where he *needed* to be and where he *wanted* to be, and was moving back home. Thank God for answered prayers and reconciliation, but those two years were painful for me in a way I didn't understand, and the unresolved pain, unbeknownst to me, festered in my young heart. It was the first time in my young life that I experienced emotional trauma, but it wasn't the last.

My older brother Randy was my hero when I was a boy. He joined the Navy and served in Operation Desert Shield, the international force that drove Saddam Hussein out of Kuwait. After the war, he was stationed in Honolulu. On March 21, 1991, he was flying off the California coast on a routine training mission in a Navy P3 submarine hunter. After their scan of the ocean, another plane came to relieve them. The second plane flew directly into my brother's plane. We never discovered if it was pilot error or if flight control had given both pilots the same altitude. A nearby helicopter reported a sudden ball of fire that sank into the ocean. No bodies were recovered.

I walked home from junior high that day, and when I arrived at our house, I saw that both of my parents' cars were in the driveway.

I knew something had happened because both of them worked and weren't ever at home when I got there in the afternoons. When I opened the front door, I saw them sitting on the sofa in the living room. They held my brother's picture, and they were trying to pray through their sobs. When I walked in, my Mom looked up and said, "Travis, it's your brother." She didn't have to explain. Somehow, I knew . . . he was gone.

I was crushed. My hero had been taken from me. I went up to my room, slammed the door, and in red hot anger prayed, "God, unless you can tell me why you killed my brother, I'll never talk to you again!"

God was silent that day, and the next, and the next. I kept my word. I turned my back on God, and for four years went on a rampage of alcohol, then drugs, and sex. I vividly remember the night I got in trouble with the law. After a wild party, I was driving home with three friends at about 2:00 a.m. when we were pulled over by the police. The officer could tell we were high, so he searched the car and found a dime bag of marijuana . . . and a pistol. We weren't in a gang, but the gangs weren't happy that we sometimes sold drugs and infringed on their territory. That's why we had a gun. In seconds, other police cars arrived. In seconds, they had the four of us face down on the pavement. They put handcuffs on us, jerked us up, and pushed us face down onto the hood of the car. Their guns were drawn and leveled on us. One of the officers put his gun at the back of my head and told me, "If you move, I'll blow your brains out!" I assumed he wasn't kidding. I looked at my three buddies only feet from me, and I had enough clarity to wonder, *I don't think this is what I signed up for when I told God*

I was done with Him! It was all a part of my pledge to reject God for being so cruel.

For the next two months after that night, God gently but clearly drew me closer. My parents prayed for me all during these troubled years, but maybe even more fervently now. God met me in my darkest moment when I was alone driving in my car. I had lost everything at this point: I lost educational opportunities when I dropped out of high school, lost important relationships, and lost the apartment I was living in. When I believed I was totally unlovable, He showered me with His affection. When I was sure my life was going nowhere, He assured me that He still had a purpose for me. When I was hopeless, He instilled a new source of hope, love, and strength. The love of God filled the car. When I got home, I walked into my parents' backyard and prayed, "God, it's me. I know I said I'd never speak to you again or serve you, but if you'll take me back, I'm yours." That was the real beginning of my faith journey.

At that moment, I stopped running from God and ran into His arms. I didn't really understand much about the gospel of grace, but I knew God was loving and forgiving—and that was enough for me at the moment. I was born again. When I embraced God's love, He healed me spiritually, but it would take time, understanding, and courage to heal the deep emotional wounds I'd experienced. I was fully "in Christ", with all the blessings of being identified with His life, His death, His resurrection, and His ascension, but working those truths deep into my heart would require the Spirit's patient love and care. Like most people, I'd never dealt with my past hurts: my parent's arguments and separation, my brother's shocking death, not being able to grieve at a funeral, the lies that led to numbing the pain with substances, and a soon-failed marriage at the tender age of eighteen, with all the heartache and confusion divorce inevitably brings. Each of these was like a sword thrust to my heart, a club breaking a bone, a vise squeezing the life out of me.

On top of all that was what crippled me the most spiritually: I got involved with Christians who had a very demanding, rules-oriented, punitive picture of God. Over and over again, I heard well-meaning leaders represent God as saying, "If you don't perform well enough, I won't love you." I didn't know how to make sense of the conflicting double message: God is loving; God is demanding and condemning. He was for me . . . but indifferent towards me? He loved me unconditionally . . . until I didn't meet His perfection conditions? He'll never leave nor forsake me . . . until I didn't pray enough to keep Him near? There were so many conflicting messages, and I lived with that gnawing, soul-sucking internal conflict for over twenty years.

It took a long time and a lot of healing to realize that my legalistic beliefs in a harsh God were just as addictive as alcohol, drugs, and sex, if not more. Addicts experience the "tolerance effect", which means their bodies adjust to the substance (or in the case of behavioral addictions like sex and gambling, the substance is dopamine, a brain chemical that produces the reward of pleasure), and they need more to get the same high. I experienced the same thing in my religious life: I performed well, which gave me a dopamine kick, but I needed to do more the next time to get the same feeling. Before long, I was as hooked on performance to earn approval as I had been on alcohol and drugs. To go back to Jesus's story of the two lost brothers in Luke 15, I had traded younger-brother addictions for an older-brother addiction. But my story is a twist on the one Jesus told. When I came home as the younger brother repenting from living a wayward life, I didn't meet the loving father on the road. . . . I met the critical, sneering older brother, and I became like him. I was working in the field—and working hard—hoping someday to be invited into the feast of the father, but no matter how much I did, it was never quite enough. (Now, as a pastor, my greatest concern is that younger brothers who come to church in need of the Father's love will meet an older brother first and completely misunderstand the nature of spiritual life, believing that the pursuit of perfection and personal performance, not the gospel, gives life.)

GOOD DEEDS AREN'T THE PROBLEM . . . TRUSTING IN THEM TO EARN GOD'S APPROVAL (AND THE APPLAUSE OF PEOPLE) IS A HUGE PROBLEM.

Jesus told the parable of the brothers precisely to illustrate the contrast between the two ways of salvation. Remember who He was talking to: younger brothers—tax collectors, pimps, prostitutes, and thieves ("sinners" by any standard) were "drawing near" to Jesus. They sensed He was different from the religious leaders. Instead of scorn and contempt, they could tell He really loved them . . . and really liked being with them! "And the Pharisees and the scribes grumbled, saying, 'This man receives sinners and eats with them'" (Luke 15:2). The story shouts to the outcasts sitting

with him, "You are a treasure to me! I love you to the skies!" And
He's telling the religious leaders, "My friends, you don't really get
it. You have the law of Moses, but you misunderstand what it's
saying. It's *not* saying you can earn God's love by strictly following
the rules. Yes, obedience is important, but it comes *after* and *as a
result of* the experience of God's love, forgiveness, and acceptance.
I once heard it said that for the holy life to be authentic, it has to
be the life we *want* to live, not the life we *have* to live. We obey
out of gratitude, not to twist God's arm to get Him to approve
of us and bless us. The Father's love embraces those who repent
from blatant sins; it also embraces those who repent from the sin
of trusting in their good record of being decent to earn what can
only be received by faith. Both keep people from the Father. Here's
the thing: the super-religious people need to repent just as much
as the pimps and prostitutes! At the end of the parable, the father
pleads with the older brother to come to the feast of salvation,
and Jesus leaves it there. But we know how the older-brother religious leaders responded: they plotted to kill Jesus, arrested him
at night, conducted a kangaroo court, and falsely accused him of
blasphemy. They delivered the Source of Life to be killed. It was
a shocking message, one that far too many self-righteous people
don't want to hear because it undercuts their primary source of
identity—their good performance.

If you've read this far in the book, God is obviously working
in your heart. You may be a younger brother who is repenting of
your bad deeds, or you may be an older brother who is repenting
of trusting in your good deeds. Good deeds aren't the problem
. . . trusting in them to earn God's approval (and the applause
of people) is a *huge* problem. We don't experience the Father's

affection by being good enough and trying harder. We enjoy the Father's welcome by saying "Yes" to His gracious invitation to the feast of salvation and remain in His extravagant love.

THINK ABOUT IT:

» *As you read this chapter, what past hurts came to mind? What have you done with those memories over the years?*

» *Of the different sources of pain, which have you suffered?*

» *Which of the brothers in Jesus's parable do you identify with most closely? Explain your answer.*

CHAPTER 20

HEALED FROM UNRESOLVED PAIN.

WE USUALLY GO TO GREAT LENGTHS TO KEEP FROM feeling pain. We try to forget the events that happened, we say it really wasn't that bad, we claim the person didn't really mean to hurt us, or we say it was "just the breaks". These attempts may deaden or allow us to evade the pain for a short time, but in the long run, the pain, fear, resentment, and shame fester deep in our hearts. We need to go back to those events—and the memories of those people—and experience God's healing touch.

Over the years I (Travis) have applied the gospel to my deepest heart wounds and studied the topic so I could teach it to others.

I've found some clear patterns. This diagram captures what I believe is how people suffer from unresolved pain—and the path to healing:

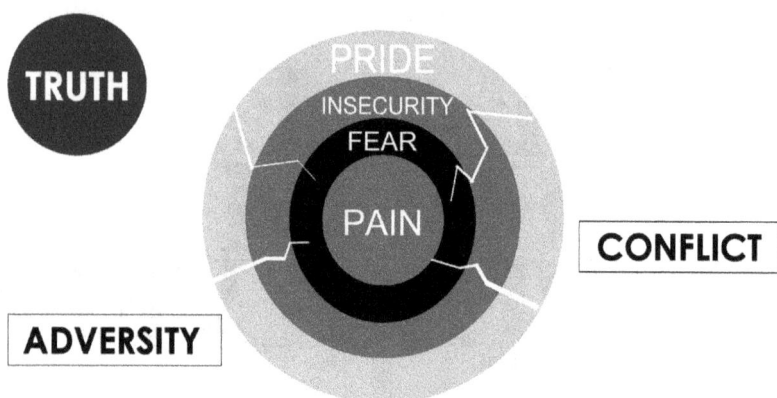

The cycle begins as unresolved pain produces fear (of being exposed, being hurt again, etc.), and then this fear creates insecurity; insecurity devolves into the pride of self-pity ("I deserve to be treated well because of how I've suffered.") or self-righteousness ("I deserve to be treated well because I'm not like those people who hurt me."), and this pride inevitably makes us fragile and vulnerable to being hurt again, so the cycle continues.

Let me go into a little more detail:

Pain

The sources of unresolved pain include a wide range of events including trauma, rejection, or different forms of abuse. We are broken people who live in a broken world. People naturally turn away from God because they don't want to change their agenda for His . . . unless and until God does the work of regeneration in their hearts. Paul described the broken condition of humans in the opening of his letter to the Romans:

> For what can be known about God is plain to them, because God has shown it to them. For his invisible attributes, namely, his eternal power and divine nature, have been clearly perceived, ever since the creation of the world, in the things that have been made. So they are without excuse. For although they knew God, they did not honor him as God or give thanks to him, but they became futile in their thinking, and their foolish hearts were darkened. Claiming to be wise, they became fools.
> —Romans 1:19-22

To some extent, all of us are wounded because we live in a fallen world.

Many of us carry hidden hurts from our childhoods. God has instituted the family as the incubator of faith, and some parents do a fabulous job of representing God to their kids. But sadly, a lot of us grew up with parents who "weren't quite good enough", and some kids were horribly abused. The imprinting of this pain in childhood will stay with us until we address it with courage and insight . . . or we die.

Some of us have suffered from catastrophic events that have traumatized us, including sexual and physical abuse, torture, floods, fires, hurricanes, the death of a parent or sibling, terrible accidents, or combat. Post-traumatic stress is debilitating and requires professional help.

Fear

When hurt is the core of our identity, we build a wall around our hearts to keep from being hurt again. Fear becomes our operating system, but we can never truly be free as long as fear is calling the shots, which covers a wide range of things that make us feel threatened, such as: the fear of failure, the fear of more rejection, the fear of losing control, the fear of not being enough, and the fear of conflict.

Insecurity

Another wall develops around our hearts, incubating that unresolved pain. Nothing will block our sense of purpose like the self-doubt of insecurity—it is an underestimated enemy of destiny. Instead of reaching forward to what God has for us to be and do, we worry that we're not competent enough, so we compare and compete with others, or we give up in hopeless despair. We work hard to mask our weaknesses, and we never want anyone to see us sweat. We keep relationships superficial, just above the point where we might reveal too much, and the person walks away.

Pride

To try to make sense of all the pain, fear, and insecurity, we trust in our own abilities, which is the essence of pride. Everyone (but us) can see it in us because we're easily offended, quickly reacting to the least perceived injustice, and we don't trust authority because we don't want anyone to hold a position over us. We blame others for our wrongs, or we blame ourselves for theirs. We lash out when someone corrects us. We may serve, but it's not open-handed; we serve to get something in return.

The principles, practices, and processes we outlined in the chapter on the family apply here. We want to briefly reiterate and reframe those points:

To wade through the layers and expose the pain, you'll need plenty of insights and courage—both, not one or the other. Insights reveal the hidden truth about what happened, and courage keeps you moving toward healing, even when the pain seems overwhelming. Our tendency, our coping strategy, is to minimize ("It wasn't that bad."), excuse ("She couldn't help it. She did the best she could do."), or deny ("It didn't hurt me at all."). Some of the most courageous people we know are those who have struggled mightily with deep emotional wounds and faulty coping strategies that only compounded the pain. These people are true heroes of the faith.

People are hurt in relationships, and they're healed in relationships. Don't try to walk this road alone. You might learn a lot of facts on your own, but you'll need a wise, patient, loving person to walk with you. There will be times when you want to quit, but this person will help you take the next step. There will be times when you want to do something that seems completely reasonable but is counterproductive, and you'll need this person to say, "Wait a minute. Let's think about this." Let us be clear: You don't need a nice person who has no clue about the healing process but is happy to give you the benefit of their advice! You need someone who has been around this block several times: a counselor, a sponsor in a group, or a friend who has been down this road and has made a lot of progress.

Trust the Holy Spirit to work. Since many of us have repressed the memories of the events that have hurt us, we may not be able to remember many of them, even when we try. We recommend that you take a significant block of time—at least an hour but probably two—to be alone and undistracted. Ask God to bring to mind the events and people who have hurt you and write them down. Most people who engage in this exercise can remember ten to fifteen pretty quickly but then hit a wall. After more time, perhaps thirty minutes, they remember a couple more, then another one and another one. After an hour and a half or two hours, they remembered things they hadn't thought about in years. In fact, some of them, particularly the last ones, may seem unimportant. Write them down anyway. Then talk through them with your counselor, sponsor, or friend. This document and this conversation will serve as the foundation for your healing and recovery.

> **YOU'RE NOT WAITING TO HEAL BEFORE GOD SEES YOU AS ENOUGH, BECAUSE YOUR WOUNDS DON'T DETERMINE YOUR WORTH—JESUS DOES.**

Be patient and persistent. Emotional, spiritual, and relational healing aren't linear. We take steps forward one day and slide back the next. New memories prompt more pain and deeper grieving. Many people say it feels like they're peeling an onion as they identify and grieve one layer of wounds at a time.

Through it all, God is with you. Jesus isn't angry at you because you're hurt, and He's not disgusted that you still struggle with it. He's tender and compassionate, and amazingly patient.

Remember: His grace is sufficient for you. You're not waiting to heal before God sees you as enough, because your wounds don't determine your worth—Jesus does. When something is damaged, it's often worth less than it was before. Perhaps that's true with cars or houses, but not with sons and daughters. Jesus didn't look at your wounds and decide that you're worthless. Instead, he declared you're worthwhile, and then He went to the cross to place your value on display for the whole world to see. You're enough right now—as you're healing and as you stumble through the messy process of allowing adversity and conflict to help break down the walls that keep you stuck in the cycle of unresolved pain.

We live in a fallen world around flawed people, so all of us get hurt, but every wound can be healed by the Great Physician.

THINK ABOUT IT:

» *Describe how fear, insecurity, and pride are the natural outworking of unhealed wounds. How do you see this cycle in the lives of people you know? (No names please, and if you write, disguise the details to protect privacy.)*

» *Take a few minutes now to ask the Holy Spirit to bring painful events and the people who caused them to mind. Don't excuse the people, don't minimize the impact of the events, and don't deny that it affected you. Write it down.*

» *Think of someone you know (maybe yourself) who has suffered significant emotional wounds. What do you think the process of healing looks like? How is it like peeling an onion? Is it worth the effort? Why or why not?*

CHAPTER 21

HEALED FROM REJECTION.

PERHAPS NOTHING HAS MORE POWER TO CONVINCE you that you're not enough like the pain of rejection. It's so important that we want to devote an entire chapter to it. Rejection runs the gamut from momentary hurt feelings to devastating betrayal and catastrophic loss. For instance . . .

Carol was the youngest of three sisters, and by her own account, the only "plain" one among them. From the time she was a little girl, her mother compared her with her beautiful older siblings, and it wasn't just their looks. Her mom praised them for their good grades in school, their athletic achievements, and their popularity. Carol had even better grades in school, but she couldn't compete with them in any other category. Day after day, her mother found fault with her. It almost seemed like a game to her mom to come up with something else to criticize, but the impact wasn't a game at all. When Carol was in junior high, she developed a strong strain of perfectionism and obsessive-compulsive disorder. She counted the tiles in the ceiling in her classrooms . . . and she counted them every day to be sure she had been accurate the day before. She made sure she didn't step on any cracks in the sidewalk on the way to and from school. She made sure she did her homework, double and triple-checked it, and did anything for extra credit. Years later when she got married, she didn't feel worthy of her husband's affection. Intimacy was a chore, and she was devastated when he pointed out any flaw In her. When they had their three children, she treated them the way her mother had treated her. It was the only way she knew to relate to them . . . or to anyone.

When Carl was a baby, the doctors discovered he had a brain bleed. They performed surgery when he was only three days old, and it seemed to solve the problem. However, the bleed came back several more times, and by the time he was ten, Carl had had six brain surgeries. A splint allowed the fluid to drain, but you can imagine how the others at school made fun of him. He suffered their jokes, and the wounds were compounded because he wasn't allowed to play sports. His condition wasn't anyone's fault, but in his high school years, he was so lonely and distraught that he looked for acceptance from the druggies. In days, he was hooked on alcohol and heroin. A brilliant student, Carl excelled in his studies even when he was high or hung over. He graduated from college and then law school, and he continued to drink and drug every day. He got married to a woman who didn't mind his addiction because he was making a lot of money, but the marriage didn't last. One day he realized his life's path was leading him to an early grave. His brain bleed and all the surgeries saved his life, but the relational consequences were more than he could handle.

When Sarah was growing up, her father was physically present but emotionally absent. She did everything she could think of to get his attention and win his affection, but nothing worked. Her mother had the same experience with him, and she tried to find meaning in perfectionism. She hoped to create a façade of "the perfect family" for people who knew them. An emotionally distant father and a perfectionistic mother caused Sarah to feel very insecure. She got the message that it wasn't acceptable to have any painful emotions like anxiety, sadness, anger, or fear. She was desperate to control something—anything—so she turned to food. At first, she used large quantities of food as substitutes for love, but as she got heavier, she despised her appearance, and she turned to binging (to get the high of being full) and purging (to be in complete control of her figure). Sarah wanted to keep her eating disorder a secret, so she tried hard to find private times and places where she could purge. She knew she was living a lie, but it was the only way she knew how to meet her powerful desires and keep her emotions under control.

BUT THE GOSPEL OF GRACE CHANGES EVERYTHING. IT GIVES US THE FOUNDATION, THE CAPABILITY, AND THE COURAGE TO FORGIVE THOSE WHO HAVE HURT US AND FIND OUR ACCEPTANCE IN CHRIST.

Travis and I have experienced our own forms of rejection, in our childhoods and in our role as pastors. Sometimes it seems that the title puts a target on our backs, and people feel free to let their criticism arrows fly! All people in the public eye are under a microscope, but some have enough security to handle unjust criticism, and a few have tough skin so it doesn't really bother them. For decades, neither Travis nor I fit in either of those boxes. Before God opened the eyes of our hearts to His grace, our insecurity made us easy marks, and even the slightest criticism . . . and even the absence of praise . . . hurt like a steel rod hitting our shins. But the gospel of grace changes everything. It gives us the foundation, the capability, and the courage to forgive those who have hurt us and find our acceptance in Christ.

As a pastor, I've sat with many wounded people. I've witnessed their pain as they've grappled with betrayal, and I do my best to step into their lives to help them. But when they instinctively cry out, "Why did this happen?", I try to avoid "reactive comforting", which is offering quick and simplistic answers to life's most difficult questions, and throwing a Bible verse at them. This response insults the person who is trying desperately to come to grips with loss, and it sends the wrong message that every devastation has a simple solution. After many years of ministry, I've learned that when a person is knocked down by rejection and other heartaches, it may sound strong to insist they get right back up, but it doesn't give space for processing the loss. That's what grieving is all about. In fact, the person's urge (and the friend's bad advice) to essentially ignore the pain compounds the hurt and creates a more serious problem: denial. Pain needs to be acknowledged, embraced, and processed before people can move on, and this takes time.

Think of yourself as a commercial passenger plane—when mechanical problems surface, the ground crew doesn't allow it to take off. Passengers may complain about the delay, but they would have a much bigger problem to gripe about on the way down in a crash! Everybody is served well by the mechanics who are doing the necessary job of fixing the problem, no matter how long it takes.

When is it a good time to acknowledge and deal with pain? Most Americans would say, "Never!" That's a problem. In fact, we look for more powerful and effective ways to avoid dealing with it, like giving in to demands, staying busy, using distractions, and avoiding the topic at all costs. We don't want to delay our flight even at the risk of an engine failure and a crash.

THINK ABOUT IT:

» *Who came to mind as you read this chapter?*
» *What is the impact of "reactive comforting"? What does it sound like? What is the real motive behind it?*

CHAPTER 22

THE PAIN AND POWER OF FORGIVENESS.

REJECTION HURTS BECAUSE IT'S PERSONAL. WE SEE THE scowling faces and we hear the condemning words—or maybe worse—people avoid us, so we feel isolated, abandoned, and excluded. Both of us have known plenty of people who let people continue to hurt them because they can't let go of the memories. We can only move on when we enter the process of forgiving the offenders. It's not easy. In fact, it reawakens the wound for a time, but it's the only sure way to be free from a painful past.

Forgiveness is God's gift to us, applied first to our own sins, and for us to apply to the sins of those who have wounded us. But forgiveness is misunderstood by so many. We need to grasp three important principles:

1) Forgiveness is our choice

A good definition of forgiveness is the intentional choice to release a person from an obligation incurred as a result of an offense committed against you. Forgiveness isn't a feeling. If we wait until we feel like forgiving, that day may never come. We forgive as an act of the will, often in spite of our feelings. Someone might ask, "Isn't forgiving someone when I don't feel like it hypocritical?" Absolutely not! Like many choices we make in following Jesus, it's an act of faith.

When we forgive, we forgive by faith. As we obey our King, we act in a way that's consistent with His character . . . and increasingly, our character. Feelings are incidental, at least at first. Over time, our feelings will probably catch up with our courageous choice to forgive. God has given us the ability to live above and beyond our feelings.

2) Forgiveness is an integral part of our new nature because it's God's nature

He would be inconsistent if He didn't forgive. Through Isaiah, the Lord assures us, "I, I am he who blots out your transgressions for my own sake, and I will not remember your sins" (Isaiah 43:25). (As a side note, when God says, "I will not remember your sins," He doesn't mean they're gone from His memory. He's omniscient; He knows all things, and He always knows all things. This term means, "I will not hold your sins against you any longer.") God forgives because it displays His heart, His honor, and His integrity.

Our ability to forgive depends on our experience of God's forgiveness. In the letter to the Ephesians, Paul makes it clear: "Let all bitterness and wrath and anger and clamor and slander be put away from you, along with all malice. Be kind to one another, tenderhearted, forgiving one another, as God in Christ forgave you" (vs. 4:31-32). Paul then explains that when we forgive, we're following the example of our loving God: "Therefore be imitators of God, as beloved children. And walk in love, as Christ loved us and gave himself up for us, a fragrant offering and sacrifice to God" (vs. 5:1-2). And the writer to the Hebrews warns, "See to it that no one fails to obtain the grace of God; that no "root of bitterness" springs up and causes trouble, and by it many become defiled" (vs. 12:15). When we cut down a tree, volunteer shoots will come up if we don't dig up the roots. That's how bitterness works: We may smile and say everything is fine, but if we don't forgive, bitterness grows deep into the soil of our hearts. So, we forgive to prevent bitterness from eating a hole in our hearts, and we forgive because our identity is "in Christ", so to withhold forgiveness is acting contrary to our true selves. Revenge seems so attractive, but actually, it's self-destructive. Author and pastor Frederick Buechner observed:

> Of the Seven Deadly Sins, anger is possibly the most fun. To lick your wounds, to smack your lips over grievances long past, to roll over your tongue the prospect of bitter confrontations still to come, to savor to the last toothsome morsel both the pain you are given and the pain you are giving back—in many ways,

it is a feast fit for a king. The chief drawback is that what you are wolfing down is yourself. The skeleton at the feast is you![30]

Bitterness has been a recurring problem for me (Ben), so I habitually ask myself these questions:

1) Am I replaying the tapes? Do I relive painful conversations, and do I anticipate the next conversation with a thirst for getting even?

2) Is my mouth out of control? When do I lose my cool? When am I critical, sarcastic, or rude?

3) Do I see the effects of bitterness in my body? Bitterness interferes with the body's hormonal and immune systems, leads to high blood pressure and increased heart rate, and is a contributing factor in a wide range of illnesses. Paul warned people of "the gall of bitterness" (Acts 8:23), which is bile—a bitter, poisonous substance that can make us sick.

4) Am I turning to anything for temporary relief? We're masters of distraction. We use all kinds of behaviors and substances to avoid thinking about our anger, hurt, and anxiety caused by our unresolved wounds. I know because I've used plenty of them.

5) Is my circle bitter? Like nasty weeds, is my bitterness spreading to other people? Do I gravitate to people who feel completely justified in their anger and resentment, and even wear it as a badge of honor? At times, Kim and our kids have absorbed some of the resentment I've brought home.

I've heard some leaders misquote passages and say with passion and conviction, "If you don't completely forgive, God won't forgive you!" Let me make three points: First, God has already

---

30 Frederick Buechner, *Wishful Thinking: A Seeker's ABC* (San Francisco: Harper One, 1993), p. 2.

forgiven you. The cross has already happened, and the complete payment has been made. You don't need to wait for it. Second, this statement misses the heart of the gospel and the order of grace and obedience: Yes, we're to forgive, but only because God has already forgiven us. True obedience is a response to the experience of grace. And third, what an incredibly unkind thing to say to someone whose child has just been killed by a drunk driver, or a woman who has been sexually abused, or anyone else who has suffered traumatic loss! They need comfort, not threats.

WE DON'T FORGIVE TO BE FORGIVEN. WE'RE FORGIVEN BECAUSE WE'VE ALREADY BEEN FORGIVEN.

In the Old Covenant, before the cross and the resurrection, forgiveness was conditional based on specific sacrifices for different kinds of offenses. But on Good Friday and Easter, the New Covenant of grace was established. Look at the stark contrasts:

The Old Covenant diagnosed the problem of sin.

The New Covenant provided the solution for sin.

The Old Covenant focused on the fear of spiritual death.

The New Covenant focuses on the spiritual life of love, hope, and power.

The Old Covenant was based on rules written on rocks.

The New Covenant creates "living stones".

The Old Covenant reveals what's wrong with us in Adam.

The New Covenant reveals what's right with us in Christ.

The Old Covenant motive for obedience was rewards.
The New Covenant motive is the love of God.
The Old Covenant prescribed what we must do.
The New Covenant describes what's already been done.
The Old Covenant required sacrifices day after day.
The New Covenant looks back at the perfect sacrifice that has already been made.

We don't forgive to be forgiven. We're forgiven because we've already been forgiven.

3) Forgiveness is for our healing

Our experience of God's forgiveness puts us in touch with His heart, and it gives us the capacity to forgive those who have hurt us. When we forgive them, we take the knife out of our own hearts and begin the healing process. As long as the knife remains stuck in us, we're hurt again every time we move. Burying the hurt without forgiving it is a short-term, ineffective fix, but it's one many of us use. Instead, we need to remember what Jesus has done for us, and this becomes our source of strength to forgive those who have hurt us. What does it mean to remember? We can think of it as re-member. The prefix means a return to a previous condition, and the main part of the word means "part of a body". So the literal meaning of "remember" is to return something to its previous condition by joining it again. For instance, if I accidentally cut my finger off, I rush to the hospital for a doctor to re-member it back onto my hand. When do we need to remember God's complete forgiveness of our sins? Speaking for myself—quite often! Every time we take the Lord's Supper, we eat the bread and drink from the cup "in remembrance" of Jesus's sacrifice. As often as you participate in the Supper, let the wonder of Jesus's sacrifice illustrated in the bread and the cup enable you to experience the reality of God's grace showered on you in Jesus.

How does forgiving the offender heal our hearts? By setting us free from the person and the event, by preventing our hearts from being contaminated by bitterness, by freeing our minds from reliving hurtful conversations and events, and by reattaching our hearts to the true source of healing power—the love, forgiveness, and acceptance freely given to us in Christ. In this way, we live out our New Covenant identity. We become in practice who we already are by faith.

Forgiveness is a process. Many people have been taught that if we choose to forgive, we'll feel instant freedom and love for the offender. I'm sure that has happened, but not often. Far more common is the experience of forgiving as much as we can as soon as we can. Thankfully, God doesn't all at once show us the full damage caused by severe abuse, betrayal, and abandonment. As we grieve and forgive one layer, he brings another to mind. This doesn't mean we haven't forgiven; it just means we haven't finished forgiving. Be both patient and tenacious in peeling back the layers until there's no unresolved wound and no unhealed pain.

HARBORING UNFORGIVENESS PROMISES THE JOY OF REVENGE, BUT QUITE OFTEN, THE ONLY ONE WHO IS HURT IS US.

Forgiveness can, but doesn't always, lead to reconciliation. Forgiveness is unilateral—we forgive whether the person is sorry, whether he even cares, whether they deserve it, and whether revenge looks more attractive than forgiving the person. But reconciliation takes both people moving toward each other. I've seen beautiful examples of this in the healing of broken marriages and strained friendships. Both sides took responsibility for their part in the rupture, and both sides made commitments to the process of rebuilding trust. Sadly, this isn't always the case, and if you're willing but the other person isn't, that's another wound to grieve and forgive. When we find the courage to speak up to someone who has hurt us and offer a path toward mending the relationship, we may be surprised that the person only wants a relationship based on their terms, just like before when you were hurt so badly. But you may also be surprised that the person is genuinely repentant, and the process of reconciliation can begin ... slowly, carefully—and with eyes wide open.

Travis and I have talked to plenty of people who have lived for years with a stronghold of unforgiveness and bitterness, and we've seen a couple of those people in the mirror. Old Covenant theology doesn't offer much help because the resources aren't strong and deep enough, but New Covenant resources are more than enough. Harboring unforgiveness promises the joy of revenge, but quite often, the only one who is hurt is us. When we withhold forgiveness, we're not hurting them, and we're not teaching them a lesson. We're only sacrificing our own joy and peace on the altar of recrimination. Refusing to forgive is like drinking poison and expecting the other person to die.

In his letter to the Romans, Paul addresses the importance of forgiveness:

> Repay no one evil for evil, but give thought to do what is honorable in the sight of all. If possible, so far as it depends on you, live peaceably with all. Beloved, never avenge yourselves, but leave it to the wrath of God, for it is written, 'Vengeance is mine, I will repay, says the Lord.' To the contrary, 'if your enemy is hungry, feed him; if he is thirsty, give him something to drink; for by so doing you will heap burning coals on his head.' Do not be overcome by evil, but overcome evil with good. —vs. 12:17-21

In the Old Testament, the law of *lex talionis*, of proportionate retribution, an eye for an eye, was given to keep conflicts from escalating. Without this law, if you took out one of my eyes, I'd want to take out both of yours! The New Covenant unplugs this law. Instead, it says, "I'm not the judge, jury, and executioner of the person who hurt me. God sits in that chair, and I need to get out of His chair!" But Paul goes further. In place of revenge, God calls us to do good to those who have hurt us—not to be foolish to let ourselves be victimized again, but from a position of strength and safety, to display the character of Christ by loving the unlovely. This, Paul explains, will have the effect of disorienting the person with love instead of hatred.

Forgiveness is the Father's precious gift to us. It costs Him the death of His Son, but He gave because of His great love for us. As we experience that love and forgiveness more deeply, we'll have the inner strength and desire to forgive those who hurt us. Forgiving them isn't excusing them, and it isn't saying it didn't hurt. It means the love of God fills us so full that we have the power to give to others at least some of what He has so lavishly given to us.

Don't be a prisoner of your past. Forgive, just as God has forgiven you.

Receiving and giving forgiveness is the only way to experience a healed heart and healed relationships.

THINK ABOUT IT:

» *Give your definition of forgiveness. What are some ways forgiveness has been misunderstood or misrepresented?*

» *How would you explain that forgiveness is both a choice and a process?*

» *What are some differences in resources and motives to forgive between the Old Covenant and the New Covenant?*

» *What's necessary for reconciliation to happen?*

» *As you read this chapter, did anyone come to mind that you need to forgive, or perhaps whose forgiveness you need to seek? If so, what's your next step?*

CHAPTER 23

HEALED FROM "NEXT."

TODAY, WE LIVE WITH A HIGHER SENSE OF URGENCY than at any time in history. Before the Industrial Revolution began in the middle of the eighteenth century, life followed the rhythms of the seasons. Most people lived on small farms, without electricity or running water, and of course, without trains, cars, and planes. And significantly, without clocks. They worked by the rising and setting of the sun and in the rhythms of the seasons, but the Industrial Revolution multiplied efficiency by the use of new technology. Over the course of a few generations, millions of people moved from farms to cities and worked in factories at demanding, fast-paced jobs. Each new wave of innovation—steam power, trains, the cotton gin, better machinery, oil, the internal combustion engine, planes, computers, the internet, and artificial intelligence, to name just a few—added more speed to the pace of life, and we learned to look at clocks and watches dozens of times a day to be sure we're "on schedule". We even walk faster today than we did a few years ago![31]

If we're committed to being healthy spiritually, emotionally, and relationally, we need to rediscover the pace of grace. I (Ben) think of my soul as a garden that needs to be tended. If I'm not patient and attentive, weeds of doubt and fear can crowd out the growing appreciation for the love of God. And if I'm not careful, a drought of neglected prayer and meditation on the Word can parch my soul. A good gardener doesn't try to rush the flowers or fruit. He trusts the normal pace of development.

An important part of slowing down to the pace of grace is (surprise!)–to be gracious to yourself. I'm a high-energy, go-for-it leader, and I burn through a lot of rocket fuel very quickly. That's not a flaw; it's my personality. But it means I need to be even more careful to slow down and pay attention to the garden of my soul. The last few years of Covid, racial unrest, economic downturns, and political upheaval have strained all of us. When I voiced my frustration, a trusted mentor told me, "Ben, we've been through a hard time . . . a really challenging time. We're all pressured, and we all need grace. Stop beating yourself up. Treat yourself with compassion."

If we don't believe we're enough, we always look into the future to determine our value. "I may not be worthy and valuable today, but someday . . ." Many of us are obsessed with "next"—the next

---

31 BBC News, "What Walking Speeds Say About Us," *BBC News*, last updated 2 May 2007, http://news.bbc.co.uk/2/hi/uk_news/magazine/6614637.stm.

promotion, the next house or car, the next award for our child, the next vacation, or the next something else. We're not satisfied with God's great grace today, and we assume fulfillment and peace are out there somewhere. In Christ, our next is now.

» Do you want to be valued? You're God's treasure.

» Do you want to belong? You're His beloved child.

» Do you want to be free from guilt and shame? "There is no condemnation for those in Christ Jesus" (Romans 8:1).

» Do you want security? Nothing can separate you from the love of God in Christ.

» Do you want significance? You're a royal priest, a representative of the King.

» Do you want to settle the fact that you're enough? Jesus is enough, and He says you're enough.

Now. Right now as you read these words. This is your inheritance, and you have it already.

Some people have called our obsession with what's next "destination addiction". Psychologist Robert Holden describes this problem:

> People who suffer from **Destination Addiction** believe that success is a destination. They are addicted to the idea that the future is where success, happiness, and heaven is. Each passing moment is merely a ticket to get to the future. They live in the "not now"; they are psychologically absent, and they disregard everything they have. Destination Addiction is a preoccupation with the idea that happiness is somewhere else. We suffer, literally, from the pursuit of happiness. We are always on the run, on the move, and on the go. Our goal is not to enjoy the day; it is to get through the day. We always have to get to somewhere else first before we can relax and before we can savor the moment.

But we never get there. There is no point of arrival. We are permanently dissatisfied.

Destination Addiction is an attempt to get on with life faster in the hope that we will enjoy our lives better. And yet our constant speeding means we frequently run past golden opportunities for grace and betterment. We are so harassed by the insecurity of our forward-seeking ego that we have no idea what it means to live by the grace of God. We seek, but we do not find. If only we could stop a while and let wisdom and grace show us a better way.[32]

One day when Kim and I were on vacation, she asked me a penetrating question, "Ben, why have you lived your entire life only to get to the end of it?"

I tried to blow her off: "What are you talking about? I don't do that."

But she was right. As I thought about her observation, I realized I'd lived at a frantic pace, exhibiting neurotic behavior. The church is full of people just like me (well, maybe not quite as bad as me, but close) who simply can't slow down and enjoy each moment as God's gracious gift. We talk about heaven, and for good reason, but I'm afraid we focus on it to the exclusion of experiencing God's presence today. Travis and I have been to countless conferences with the word "next" in the title, and we've read dozens of books about reaching this or that goal. Those aren't wrong or evil . . . unless we miss the joy of the present moment of basking in the love of God. Trigger-happy prophets have used the word *next* to put pressure on people to follow their lead. If we listen long enough and intently enough, we can easily feel

32 Robert Holden, Ph.D., "What Is Destination Addiction? How to Stop Thinking about What Comes Next," *Robert Holden, Ph.D. Blog*, https://www.robertholden.com/blog/what-is-destination-addiction/.

that we're not enough until we meet their expectations—and we lose focus on being enough in Christ. We're here to tell you that you're not waiting for next to be enough—you're enough now through Christ.

Jesus bore the eternal destiny of every human being—a crushing weight—but we never see Him in a hurry, never frantic, never frustrated by the pace of things. When he says, "Follow me," at least part of that means to go at His pace alongside Him, not run ahead of Him to achieve or acquire more.

Yes, we need a vision. Jesus had a clear vision of a desired future. Yes, we need a plan. Jesus was born to inaugurate the new Kingdom of the crucified and risen Messiah. Yes, we need commitment and tenacity. Jesus "set His face like flint" to go to Jerusalem to take the punishment we deserve so we could experience the honor He deserves. But in all these pursuits, Jesus kept His heart fixed on the Father, spending long times in prayer and walking (not running) from place to place.

Today, many of us suffer from "hurry sickness". We check our watches incessantly, get frustrated if the car in front of us doesn't immediately go when the light turns green, rush to complete tasks, and live with a nagging sense of FOMO—fear of missing out. An article in *Forbes* describes the problem:

> Achieving, growing, and performing better in every single sphere requires hard work and time investment. Getting things done feels good and rewards our brain with a hit of dopamine. Being busy and making full use of our talents and resources to achieve excellence is desirable. But when busyness tips over into a "hurry sickness", our body starts releasing the stress hormone cortisol, which can long-term cause depression. In a constant

state of overstimulation, our minds make us also feel tired, anxious, prone to irritability, and unable to relax. Time is a finite source. And unfortunately, non-renewable. Consequently, we end up going through life unconsciously in our busy way of running around.[33]

Jesus came to give us an abundant life, not to rush us to an end. In Him, we're *beloved*, so we need to allow ourselves to experience *being loved* by God. Our job isn't to achieve God's presence and affection but to put ourselves in a posture to continually receive what He has already given. In our pursuit of "next", we may find Jesus to be more useful than beautiful—we trust Him to make us more effective and give us blessings—but we miss the wonder of His awesome power and love. Wonder shouldn't be uncommon in our hearts and in our worship. After Peter spoke at Pentecost and three thousand believed, Luke tells us, "And awe came upon every soul, and many wonders and signs were being done through the apostles" (Acts 2:43).

Destination addiction is devoid of wonder. It looks down at what I have to get done right away, and it looks forward to a time when all my efforts will finally pay off, but it doesn't look up to see the beauty of Jesus. It causes us to miss the joys of relating to our spouse, children, and friends, and the simple pleasures that God surrounds us with every single day. King David was a busy man—ruling a nation, commanding an army in battle, administrating the kingdom—but he knew the source of peace in the midst of chaos: "One thing have I asked of the Lord, that will I seek after: that I may dwell in the house of the Lord all the days

33 Paloma Cantero-Gomez, "Ten Intelligent Ways to Combat Your Hurry Sickness," *Forbes*, 1 February 2019, https://www.forbes.com/sites/palomacanterogomez/2019/02/01/ten-intelligent-ways-to-combat-your-hurry-sickness/?sh=a28c681572e4.

of my life, to gaze upon the beauty of the Lord and to inquire in his temple" (Psalm 27:4).

> **WHEN WE SLOW DOWN AND LET THE BEAUTY OF GOD FILL OUR HEARTS, WE STRIVE, BUT FOR A VERY DIFFERENT REASON.**

He had many responsibilities, but "one thing" was most important. What was it? To "dwell", inhabit, and occupy the place where heaven and earth meet. When? "All the days of my life." And what happened there? David gazed, which is a prolonged stare, at "the beauty of the Lord" and interacted with God about the things that concerned him.

I have to ask, "Is God beautiful to me? Is He a means to my success, or is He the end, my highest good, my treasure, my delight?" How about you?

Here are some questions that help me "inquire in his temple":

» Do I expect the next big success, big purchase, or big event will finally give me the significance and peace I long for?

» How much do I look around at others and wonder why I'm not farther ahead?

» How much energy am I expending on a dream of the future at the expense of delighting in God today (and my family and friends today)?

Kim's question started me on this journey, and it prompted new insights and changes.

We need to reframe our days and weeks to carve out time to delight in God, and we need to do the harder work of reframing our hearts so that we aren't frantic all day every day. The change will be difficult because our culture screams that we have to hurry even more! We can get off the runaway freight train of destination addiction only when we realize we're *living from* a secure place of security and significance instead of *striving for* security and significance. "Next" is an attractive but empty promise. When we slow down and let the beauty of God fill our hearts, we strive, but for a very different reason. In Paul's letter to the Colossians, he explained, "Him we proclaim, warning everyone and teaching everyone with all wisdom, that we may present everyone mature in Christ. For this I toil, struggling with all his energy that he powerfully works within me" (vs. 1:28-29).

If anything, an experience of grace sharpens our vision because we're more in tune with God's heart for the lost and the least, and it gives us a different kind of energy because we tap into His limitless resources in the Spirit instead of "running on empty".

We can't add anything to our status as God's forgiven, righteous, adopted children. One more accolade won't add to it, or one more possession, or one more promotion, or one more dollar. It's done. It's over. Our standing with the God of the universe is secure and complete. Jesus said, "It is finished," "It is paid"—the struggle is over.

My (Travis's) doctoral professor, Gary Moon asked me some questions to help me grasp the Father's heart. He asked, "Travis, do you have kids?"

"Yes, I sure do."

"Do you have a backyard where they play?"

"Yes."

"Do you ever watch them play, smiling and laughing?"

"Of course. I love it."

"At what point as you watch them do you say to yourself, 'Gosh, I sure hope they know what they're doing. I hope they get it right.'"

"Uh . . . never."

Gary then told me, "That's the way it is with the Father. He doesn't look at you and wonder if you're going to get it right. He wants to know if you're really enjoying the life He's given you."

We know that the enemy of our souls doesn't want us to live at the pace of grace. He wants us to stay on the treadmill of performance, searching and striving toward a destination that's always just out of reach. Scripture gives us a unique glimpse into the strategy of the enemy to keep us addicted to a destination. Daniel received a prophetic word about the Son of Man, but he also received a warning: The enemy "shall speak words against the Most High, and shall wear out the saints of the Most High, and shall think to change the times and the law" (Daniel 7:24-25). This is a clear warning against our preoccupation with "next". It's based on the lie that God's timing is too slow and His grace isn't enough, which leaves us driven or depressed (or both) and wears us out. Satan speeds up the clock, making us feel that we're always behind, and fooling us that we're still under the law which condemns. Fatigue drains our faith, and we're more easily tempted when we're tired and frustrated. The enemy whispers, "Oh gosh, you're behind. What's wrong with you? You'd better hurry to make up for lost time!" Instead of enjoying the moment, our focus is riveted on the only thing that seems important: catching up. We believe our lives are valuable only in our accomplishments, and the quicker the better. We worry and we hurry, but no matter how much we get checked off our to-do sheets, we can easily miss the blessings of God and the abundance.

When the Spirit shows us where we've missed God's best, we have a choice: to ignore the Spirit's whisper, kick against it by being defensive, grovel in self-condemnation for being such a bad Christian, or grasp the opportunity to change our agenda to align with God's. Throughout this book, we've tried to highlight a number of ways we may have missed God's best. We hope the Spirit of God has been drawing you close, convincing you that His grace is the only foundation for life, and celebrating your new choices to bathe your mind, heart, and soul in God's magnificent grace. That's our hope. That's our prayer.

Experience freedom from bondage to "next". God's grace is enough, and in Him, you're enough.

THINK ABOUT IT:

» *How would you define "destination addiction"?*

» *What are some symptoms of it? What are the promises and justifications we use to continue to believe it's true?*

» *What's the promise of "hurry sickness"? Why is it a sickness and not a virtue?*

» *What would the pace of grace look like for you? For your family?*

» *As you read this book, what insights and revelations has God given you? How are you responding to them? What difference will they make over time?*

FIFTY "I AM" STATEMENTS

Below are fifty things you need to know about your new God-given identity. Read these 344 words out loud, with conviction, and I guarantee you it will leave you feeling encouraged . . . and new! These can also be found online at bendailey.com/if-anyone-is-in-christ-he-is-a-new-creation/.

I AM

- » I am a saint, a trophy of Christ's victory. (Romans 1:7, Ephesians 1:1, Philippians 1:1 Jude 1:3; 2 Corinthians 2:14, AMP)
- » I am born again of imperishable seed. (1 Peter 1:23)
- » I am a new creation, complete in Christ and perfect forever. (2 Corinthians 5:17; Colossians 2:10; Hebrews 10:14)

» I am a child of God, the apple of my Father's eye. (1 John 3:1; Psalm 17:8)

» I am one with the Lord and the temple of the Holy Spirit. (1 Corinthians 6:17; 1 Corinthians 6:19)

» I am eternally redeemed and completely forgiven. (Hebrews 9:12; Colossians 2:13)

» I am seated with Christ in heavenly realms. (Ephesians 2:6)

» I am summoned by name and I am His. (Isaiah 43:1, 2 Corinthians 1:22)

» I am dead to sin and alive to God. (Romans 6:11)

» I am free from guilt and condemnation. (Hebrews 10:22, Romans 8:1)

» I am righteous, holy, and blameless! (2 Corinthians 5:21; Ephesians 1:4)

» I am healed and I am strong in the Lord. (1 Peter 2:24; Ephesians 6:10)

» I am hidden in Christ and eternally secure. (Colossians 3:3; Hebrews 6:19)

» I am loved with an everlasting love and I am highly favored. (Jeremiah 31:3; Ephesians 1:6, *charitto*)

» I am my Beloved's and He is mine. (Songs of Solomon 6:3)

» I am the head and not the tail. (Deuteronomy 28:13)

» I am blessed with every spiritual blessing and I am a joint heir with Christ. (Ephesians 1:3; Romans 8:17)

» I am a competent minister of the New Covenant. (2 Corinthians 3:6)

» I am bona fide and qualified, chosen, and anointed. (Colossians 1:12; John 15:8, Colossians 3:12, 1 Thessalonians 1:4, 1 Peter 2:9; 1 John 2:27)

- » I am His royal ambassador, a missionary to the world. (2 Corinthians 5:20; Matthew 28:19)
- » I am a stranger on earth, a citizen of a city whose maker is God. (Hebrews 11:13; Hebrews 11:10, 16, 12:22)
- » I am not looking back but I am pressing on to know Him more. (Philippians 3:14)
- » I am trusting that He will finish in me that which He started. (Hebrews 12:2, Jude 1:24, 2 Corinthians 9:8)
- » I am a king and a priest, a carrier of the Lord's authority. (Revelation 1:6; Luke 10:19)
- » I am a healer of the sick and a demon's worst nightmare. (Mark 16:18; Matthew 10:8)
- » I am king o' the world because His victory is mine! (1 John 5:4; 1 Corinthians 15:57)
- » I am as bold as a lion and more than a conqueror. (Proverbs 28:1; Romans 8:37)
- » I am a towering testimony of the Spirit's power. (1 Corinthians 2:4, 12:7, 2 Corinthians 1:9)
- » I am the salt of the earth and the light of the world. (Matthew 5:13; Matthew 5:14)
- » I am the sweet smell of Jesus to those who are perishing. (2 Corinthians 2:15)
- » I am a tree planted by the water, and I am a fruitful branch. (Psalm 1:3, Jeremiah 17:7; John 15:8)
- » I am the disciple whom Jesus loves. (Ephesians 1:6)
- » And by the grace of God, I am what I am. (1 Corinthians 15:10)

RESOURCES

» GCCM: www.GCCM.cc
» Gospel Institute: www.GospelInstitute.cc
» Leadership Institute for Core Development: cultivatemypurpose.com
» Transformational Truths Podcast
» Calvary Church: www. CalvaryChurch.cc
» TedTalk: The Dangers of Unresolved Pain
» 50 "I Am" Statements: www.bendailey.com/if-anyone-is-in-christ-he-is-a-new-creation/
» BenDailey.com

www.ingramcontent.com/pod-product-compliance
Lightning Source LLC
Chambersburg PA
CBHW062053080426
42734CB00012B/2639

* 9 7 8 1 9 5 7 3 6 9 6 2 4 *